TEACHING FAMILY REUNIFICATION

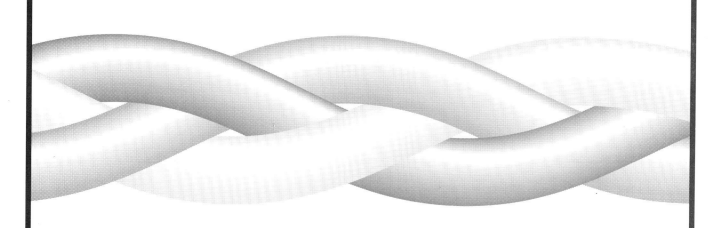

A SOURCEBOOK

Robin Warsh, Anthony N. Maluccio, Barbara A. Pine

The Child Welfare League of America • Washington, DC

CHILD WELFARE LEAGUE OF AMERICA, INC.
440 First Street, NW, Suite 310, Washington, DC 20001-2085

CURRENT PRINTING (last digit)
10 9 8 7 6 5 4 3 2 1

Cover design by Jennifer Riggs
Text design by Eve Malakoff-Klein

Printed in the United States of America

ISBN # 0–87868–511–1

Family reunification...

is the planned process of reconnecting children in out-of-home care with their families by means of a variety of services and supports to the children, their families, and their foster parents or other service providers. It aims to help each child and family to achieve and maintain, at any given time, their optimal level of reconnection—from full reentry of the child into the family system to other forms of contact, such as visiting, that affirm the child's membership in the family.

 Contents

 *Foreword*

With increased media attention to the voices of children in out-of-home care, their families, and their foster families, the American public has begun to appreciate the dilemmas that child welfare professionals have been experiencing firsthand for decades. How can we preserve families and at the same time protect endangered children from harm? What constitutes "good-enough" parenting? How do we weigh the risks of returning children to their families against the risks of a prolonged stay in out-of-home care? And while we support the rehabilitation of biological families, as stressed in the federal Adoption Assistance and Child Welfare Act of 1980 (P.L. 96–272), *how* do we do it well? The field has been asking, with urgency, for direction on safe methods to attempt, effect, and maintain reunification once family problems have become sufficiently severe to warrant placement out of the home.

Through the publication of *Teaching Family Reunification: A Sourcebook*, the authors have made an impor-

tant contribution to the theory and practice of family reunification. They have synthesized a philosophical approach, a set of principles and guidelines, and a series of teaching activities and resources that provide an avenue to put into practice social work's respect for the powerful and lasting meaning of families to human beings.

Changes in service delivery systems required by the challenges of family reunification include the need for highly-trained staff. For a decade, Robin Warsh, Anthony Maluccio, and Barbara Pine have worked as a team to develop child welfare education and training materials. Since 1992, their project has been conducted through the Graduate School of Social Work at Boston College.

We are pleased to support their work and salute this latest effort to help agencies and schools respond to the needs of children and families who are served by the child welfare system.

JUNE GARY HOPPS, DEAN
Boston College
Graduate School of Social Work

 *Preface*

Teaching Family Reunification: A Sourcebook is one outcome of a two-year project, conducted from September 1988 to December 1990 at the University of Connecticut School of Social Work, to produce a range of training materials on family reunification through collaboration between child welfare agencies and schools of social work.*

The major vehicle for collaboration was the New England Consortium on Family Reunification, convened by project staff and comprising representatives of six state child welfare agencies in New England, 15 schools or departments of social work (also in New England), Casey Family Services, and other interested agencies and organizations. Their involvement and guidance helped implement the project and reinforced the staff's conviction that the preparation of competent family-centered child welfare practitioners and administrators is best accomplished when there is continuing interaction between agencies and schools in the development of educational materials and approaches.

A major purpose of the project was to develop and disseminate teaching materials for use by social work educators and agency trainers. *Teaching Family Reunification: A Sourcebook* helps fulfill this purpose by providing the conceptual tools to rethink family reunification, setting forth the range of competencies required for effective family reunification practice, presenting curriculum modules aimed at enhancing competence in family reunification theory and practice, and compiling a comprehensive bibliography.

*   "Promoting Family Reunification through Agency-School Collaboration," a project funded by the U.S. Department of Health and Human Services, Office of Human Development Services, Administration for Children, Youth and Families (Grants No. 90-CW-0942/01 and 02) and The Annie E. Casey Foundation (1988–1990).

×

Acknowledgments

In working on *Teaching Family Reunification: A Sourcebook*, we were privileged to collaborate with many individuals and organizations interested in the area of family reunification. We are deeply grateful for their generosity and commitment to the goals of the project. They include the U.S. Department of Health and Human Services, Office of Human Development Services, Administration for Children, Youth and Families and The Annie E. Casey Foundation, which jointly funded the project; and the New England Consortium on Family Reunification, which provided invaluable guidance to project staff. Members of the Consortium include:

- Ray Barrett, New Hampshire Division for Children and Youth Services;

- Lynn Boyle, Social and Rehabilitation Services, State of Vermont;

- Beverly C. Burke, Connecticut Department of Children and Families;

- George W. Caulton, Western New England College;

- Michael Chuse, Castleton State College;

- Mary M. Danna, Salve Regina College;

- Vincent E. Faherty, University of Southern Maine;

- Edith Fein, Casey Family Services;

- Ann Hartman, Smith College;

- Michie Hesselbrock, Southern Connecticut State University;

- Robert Jolley, University of New Hampshire;

- Sara Kobylenski, Casey Family Services;

- Jean McCandless, Social and Rehabilitation Services, State of Vermont;

- Minou Michlin, Southern Connecticut State University;

- Scott Mueller, Rhode Island College;

- Leroy Pelton, Salem State College;

- Freda Plumley, Maine Department of Child and Family Services;

- Bruce Rollins, Rhode Island Department of Children, Youth and Families;

- Susan Rosen, U.S. Department of Health and Human Services, Region I;

- Marguerite Rosenthal, Salem State College;

- Paula Schneider, Regis College;

- David Sherwood, Gordon College;

- Sau-Fong Siu, Wheelock College;

- Greg Sorozan, Massachusetts Department of Social Services;

- Pamela Stockwell, Rhode Island College;

- Julie Sweeney-Springwater, Massachusetts Department of Social Services;

- Gail Werrbach, University of Maine at Orono;

In addition to Consortium members, project staff members consulted with a range of experts on family reunification and related areas, each of whom contributed to this publication by reviewing earlier drafts and field-testing portions of these materials. We are especially grateful to the following:

- Marcia Allen, National Resource Center on Family Based Services, University of Iowa;

- Rosemarie Carbino, University of Wisconsin–Madison;

- Paul Carlo, Center on Child Welfare, University of Southern California School of Social Work (formerly with Five Acres–The Boys' and Girls' Society of Los Angeles);

- James Carr, Connecticut Department of Children and Families;

- Inger Davis, San Diego State University;

- Wendy Deutelbaum, National Resource Center on Family Based Services, University of Iowa;

- Joy Duva, Casey Family Services, Shelton, CT;

- Judith Elkin, Talbot Perkins Children's Services, New York, NY;

- Martha Jones, Common Sense Associates, Inc., Mechanicsburg, PA;

- Kathleen Olmstead, retired, formerly with Child and Family Services, Hartford, CT;

- Elizabeth M. Tracy, Mandel School of Applied Social Sciences, Case Western Reserve, Cleveland, OH;

- Diane Yost, formerly with the Illinois Department of Children and Family Services, Chicago, IL;

- Jeanne Zamosky, Familystrength, Concord, NH;

For their interest and encouragement, we also thank Martin Schwartz, formerly Director of The Annie E. Casey Foundation; Lucille Tomanio, Executive Director, Casey Family Services; Nancy Humphreys, Dean, University of Connecticut School of Social Work; and Phyllis Nophlin and Beatrice Moore, Project Officers, U.S. Department of Health and Human Services, Administration for Children, Youth and Families. We thank Pam Day of the Child Welfare League of America for her careful review of an earlier version of this book. Her suggestions helped us make the curriculum modules more useful to trainers and strengthened the connection between family reunification competencies and training.

We are especially grateful to Pamela Harrison, Senior Secretary for the project, for her outstanding professionalism, effectiveness, and commitment, and to Elisa Taylor, who readily helped us to complete this manuscript while Pamela was on leave. And to Beth Nichols and Debra Waz, of Wordflow, we owe a debt of gratitude for pulling all the strands together into one piece.

Since August of 1992, our work in the area of family reunification has been conducted through Boston College Graduate School of Social Work, which two of us joined on a full-time basis. We wish to thank Dean June Gary Hopps for her warm welcome and support.

A number of persons have contributed to this *Sourcebook* by generously sharing their work with us. We are grateful to Peg McCartt Hess, Columbia University School of Social Work, and Kathleen Ohman Proch, University of Denver School of Social Work, authors of *Family Visiting in Out-of-Home Care: A Guide to Practice*. We have drawn from that publication to design the set of training activities and accompanying handouts contained in Module IV.

We are also indebted to Gail Folaron, Indiana University School of Social Work, who has used a decade of rich experience with children in placement to construct a set of guidelines and practice approaches for preparing children to reconnect with their families. Practitioners will no doubt benefit from her material as they are exposed to new ways of helping children through the reunification process.

Edith Fein, Casey Family Services, has contributed much in the area of assessment and goal planning in family reunification. We appreciate her sharing her work on the use of clear goal statements; linkages among goals, family strengths, and resources; action plans for effecting and maintaining family reconnections; and the Parker-Vega case.

Vincent E. Faherty, University of Southern Maine, developed the case study of the Cooper Family, an Iowa case that received much publicity in the late 1980s and on which a made-for-television movie was based. This case, and related discussion questions and learning activities, help to highlight and reinforce the material presented in the preceding curriculum modules.

Portions of the modules in this *Sourcebook* have been tested in workshops and in graduate social work courses, and we appreciate the feedback we have received from participants. We would also be grateful for ideas and suggestions from trainers and educators as they tailor these materials for use in their own programs.

Finally, we wish to thank the many agency administrators and practitioners who spoke to us of the keen challenges they face in helping to restore families—of their enormous responsibilities and severely limited resources. Their messages shaped and reshaped the materials in this *Sourcebook* as well as our other publications. We owe them, and their clients, a debt of gratitude.

ROBIN WARSH
ANTHONY N. MALUCCIO
BARBARA A. PINE

About the Authors

Robin Warsh was the Director of the Project on Family Reunification, of which this publication is one outcome. She is currently Project Director of "Preserving Families Through Reunification" at Boston College Graduate School of Social Work. The project, funded by The Annie E. Casey Foundation, will produce a guide for use by child welfare agencies to assess and improve their capacity to reunify children in placement with their families. She teaches and writes in the areas of family reunification and independent living for adolescents in foster care.

Anthony N. Maluccio was the project's Principal Investigator. He is Professor of Social Work and Chair of the Doctoral Program at Boston College School of Social Work. During the time that this book was written, he was Professor at the University of Connecticut School of Social Work and Director of its Center for the Study of Child Welfare. He teaches and writes extensively in the areas of casework, research, and family and children's services.

Barbara A. Pine was the Curriculum Specialist on the project. She is Associate Professor at the University of Connecticut School of Social Work. She teaches and writes in the areas of child welfare policy and practice, ethics, and social work administration, and provides consultation to public and private child welfare agencies.

Each year in the United States, many of the children in family foster care, group homes, or residential treatment centers are reunited with their families. In 1990, the latest year for which comprehensive national data are available, 66% of the children who left care were discharged to their biological families [Tatara 1993]. Sooner or later, however, a substantial proportion of these children return to some form of out-of-home placement or enter a more restrictive setting, such as a correctional facility for juveniles or a psychiatric hospital [Fein et al. 1983; Pine et al. 1993; Rzepnicki 1987]. Meanwhile, many other children in out-of-home care continue to wait for reunification [Fein et al. 1990]. In response to the needs and experiences of these children and their families, there has been a marked increase in recent years in efforts to apply principles and strategies of intensive family preservation services (IFPS) to case situations involving family reunification.

Intensive efforts to reconnect families separated by the placement of their children in out-of-home care and to keep them together after reconnection are similar in many ways to those designed to prevent placement. Foremost is their shared purpose: strengthening and enhancing families. Other similarities include the provision of concrete as well as intangible services and supports in the family's own home by accessible staff who work flexible hours. Attention is paid to the family as a system to strengthen family bonds, link family members with formal and informal resources, and help parents improve their child care skills [Whittaker et al. 1990].

At the same time, family preservation services aimed at reunifying families differ from those designed to prevent placement in a number of significant ways:

- Workers must address the typically traumatic impact that loss and separation have on the placed child as well as on the parents and other family members.

- In many instances, contact between children in placement and their parents may need to be reestablished before family bonds can be strengthened.

- The practitioner and the family face different challenges in teaching and learning parenting skills when children are out of the home than are faced in intensive family preservation efforts.

- The sense of crisis present when a family is threatened by the imminent removal of a child is not present in family reunification situations.

- Parents whose child has been placed may be perceived by themselves and others as having "failed"; therefore, fostering hope and a belief in competence and the potential for success presents a greater challenge in work with families who have experienced placement than in work with those who have not.

- During placement, a child may have formed a relationship with a caregiver, such as a foster parent, that will need to be recognized and dealt with by parent and child.

- Reunification services may have to be provided for a much longer term than is the case for IFPS.

These differences pose special challenges for child welfare administrators and staff, as well as for the full range of professionals involved in reunifying families, including foster parents, therapists, attorneys, and judges. For example, agency staff members and foster parents need to recognize the importance of family visiting as an opportunity to assess family functioning and promote positive change. Administrators and judges must create policies that support appropriate forms of family reunification other than return home. Therapists have to be particularly attuned to opportunities to promote family functioning. And all service providers need to be specialists, that is, trained to meet the special needs of families on the path toward reunification [Pine et al. 1993].

Teaching Family Reunification: A Sourcebook contributes to the development of well-trained service providers working on family reunification by providing a four-part resource for training and educating child welfare personnel.

Part 1, *Rethinking Family Reunification*, provides an expanded definition of family reunification and a set of underlying principles and guidelines for practice, describes agency supports needed to promote effective practice and service delivery, discusses competency-based education and training, and examines a sample of various child welfare issues and dilemmas that affect family reunification practice.

Part 2, *Family Reunification Competencies for Social Workers,* delineates the knowledge, attitudes, and skills necessary for successfully reunifying families. The competencies are organized into five major parts, following the process of family reconnection:

1. Practitioners commit themselves to a set of values and attitudes that will guide their practice.

2. Practitioners evaluate the family's readiness to reunify.

3. Practitioners use the results of the assessment to formulate goals and service agreements.

4. Practitioners work directly with children and parents and collaborate with other service providers.

5. Practitioners prepare the family to remain connected, end the service, and evaluate their work.

Part 3, *Curriculum Modules for Teaching Family Reunification,* comprises five curriculum modules on increasing competence in family reunification. Modules I through III have been designed for two- to three-hour sessions and focus on the interrelated concepts of the expanded definition of family reunification, the opportunities and hazards inherent in the process of collaboration among providers that is so necessary a part of reunification practice, and the development of model policies and programs to support family reunification. Module IV focuses extensively on child and family visiting; its five units take eight hours to complete. Module V includes a detailed case study and related discussion questions, learning activities, and references through which many of the themes presented in the *Sourcebook* can be further explored and understood. *Handouts* are included at the end of each module to reinforce the teaching opportunities presented and to provide directions for practice exercises that will help participants expand their learning through experiential activities. The handouts may be copied and distributed for classroom or training purposes.

Part 4, *Selected References,* includes bibliographies on child welfare, competency-based training in child welfare, family reunification, family preservation, permanency planning, race and ethnicity, child maltreatment, adoption, group care/residential treatment, family foster care, and adolescents and independent living.

Teaching Family Reunification: A Sourcebook is intended for use by service providers working toward reunification of families with their children. This statement is intentionally broad because it is based on a recognition that these families have needs that must be understood by a full range of providers, whether these providers are employed in a specialized reunification program, a private foster care setting, or a public child welfare agency. Our target audience includes workers handling generic caseloads, family reunification specialists, case managers, and foster parents. In addition, the material is highly relevant to others whose careful work with families on the road to reunification is central, including judges, attorneys, substance abuse counselors, and parent aides.

The information presented in this book can be used in a variety of ways, such as in agency staff development programs, in continuing education programs, and in schools of social work. Because reunification work is tied directly to the judicial system, these materials can also be used in schools of law and in continuing education programs for attorneys and judges. Each curriculum module may be used by itself (adapted to the particular needs of students or trainees) or in conjunction with a broader training or educational activity. For example, an undergraduate or graduate social work program might integrate the modules into practice courses or specialized courses in the area of family and children's services. Child welfare agencies might use the individual modules as part of orientation sessions, or integrate the complete set of modules into the agency's ongoing in-service training plan. In addition, *Teaching Family Reunification: A Sourcebook* makes an excellent companion to *Together Again: Family Reunification in Foster Care,* edited by the *Sourcebook* authors. *Together Again,* which includes chapters by the authors as well as other social work educators, researchers, and practitioners, focuses on the establishment and implementation of family reunification programs and can enhance the learner's appreciation of family reunification theory and practice.

The material described in this book is specialized—it goes beyond the generic interviewing, assessment, and goal planning knowledge and skills required for competent social work practice. To effectively use the training opportunities described, participants must already have a basic body of knowledge and skills on which to build. The materials presented in this *Sourcebook* are best used in a competency-based or performance-based approach to education and training.

References

Fein, E.; Maluccio, A.N.; Hamilton, V.J.; and Ward, D.E. "After Foster Care: Outcomes of Permanency Planning for Children." *Child Welfare* LXII, 6 (November–December 1983): 485–562.

Fein, E.; Maluccio, A.N.; and Kluger, M. *No More Partings— An Examination of Long-Term Foster Family Care.* Washington, DC: Child Welfare League of America, 1990.

Pine, B.A.; Warsh, R.; and Maluccio, A.N., eds. *Together Again: Family Reunification in Foster Care.* Washington, DC: Child Welfare League of America, 1993.

Rzepnicki, T.L. "Recidivism of Foster Children Returned to Their Own Homes: A Review and New Directions for Research." *Social Service Review* 61, 1 (March 1987): 56–70.

Tatara, T. *Characteristics of Children in Substitute and Adoptive Care. A Statistical Summary of the VCIS National Child Welfare Database—Based on FY82 through FY90 Data.* Washington, DC: American Public Welfare Association, 1993, p. 73.

Whittaker, J.K.; Kinney, J.; Tracy, E.M.; and Booth, C., eds. *Reaching High-Risk Families: Intensive Family Preservation in Human Services.* New York: Aldine de Gruyter, 1990.

PART I

RETHINKING FAMILY REUNIFICATION: GUIDELINES FOR POLICY, PROGRAM, PRACTICE, AND TRAINING

- *Redefinition*
- *Underlying Principles and Guidelines*
- *The Agency Context*
- *A Competency-Based Approach to Education and Training*
- *Recurring Issues and Dilemmas*

Rethinking Family Reunification

Family reunification has long been an integral part of out-of-home care practice; it is often viewed as the desired outcome of out-of-home placement of children and youths. Successful family reunification, however, requires a full range of efforts that are supported by well-grounded theory and that target and respond to the needs of children and their families.

Redefinition

Family reunification practice traditionally has been based on the premise that children and youths in out-of-home care needed to be either returned to their families of origin or placed in another setting intended to be permanent. This either-or orientation has long been supported, and in some ways required, by the policy and legal framework of child welfare practice. All too often, termination of parental rights has been sought when families have been unable to care for children in their home, even when no other permanent family has been, or is likely to be, found for the children.

It is time to challenge this premise as too simplistic and not responsive to the qualities and situations of families whose children are in out-of-home care. Instead, social workers, attorneys, judges, and other service providers must rethink family reunification and see it as a flexible, dynamic approach that seeks to meet the needs of children and their families in an individualized and carefully thought-through way. Accordingly, an expanded definition of family reunification is needed:

> *Family reunification is the planned process of reconnecting children in out-of-home care with their families by means of a variety of services and supports to the children, their families, and their foster parents or other service providers. It aims to help each child and family to achieve and maintain, at any given time, their optimal level of reconnection—from full reentry of the child into the family system to other forms of contact, such as visiting, that affirm the child's membership in the family.*[1]

This expanded view of family reunification underscores the value of maintaining and enhancing connectedness or reconnectedness between children in out-of-home care and their families or members of their extended kinship system. At the same time, it recognizes that not every parent can be a daily caregiver and that some families, though not able to live together, can still maintain kinship bonds. This redefinition of reunification must be accompanied by an expanded definition of *family*; the terms *parents* and *families* are used in a generic sense in this *Sourcebook* to refer to those parents or caregivers who are *meaningful* to the child and with whom family reunification is being considered. While for the most part this refers to biological parents or families, reconnections can also include adoptive parents and families, grandparents, primary caregivers, or other significant attachment figures the child may have, including foster parents. The implications for changes in social work and legal practice of these expanded definitions will be explored throughout this *Sourcebook*.

Underlying Principles and Guidelines

Redefining family reunification leads to a number of principles that can guide family reunification policies, programs, practices, and training, including the following:

1. Family reunification is an integral part of the philosophy of preserving families and of permanency planning, with their emphasis on ensuring continuity of care for children. Family reunification should be systematically considered and planned for by the child welfare and legal systems as early as possible in a child's placement in out-of-home care.

2. Family reunification is a dynamic process that must be based on the child's and family's changing qualities, needs, and potentialities. It should be viewed by all who provide services to the family as a continuum, with levels or outcomes ranging from full reentry into the family system to partial reentry to less

extensive contact. At any point during the child's placement in out-of-home care, the most appropriate or optimal level of reconnection should be identified and actively pursued. This philosophy and practice should be recognized and supported by the judicial system. At the same time, it should be recognized that reconnection is not possible or desirable in some situations, and that those situations may appropriately require termination of parental rights. Even in such instances, however, children should at the least be helped to move into new permanent families with some tangible tie to their past in the form of pictures, a lifebook, or other family memorabilia.

3. As a form of preserving families, reunification embodies (a) conviction about the role of the biological family as the preferred child-rearing unit, if at all possible; (b) recognition of the potential of most families to care for their children, if properly assisted; (c) awareness of the impact of separation and loss on children and parents; and (d) involvement, as appropriate, of any and all members of the child's family, including members of the extended family or others who, while not legally related, are considered by the child and themselves to be "family."

4. Reunification practice is guided by an ecologically oriented, competence-centered perspective that emphasizes promoting family empowerment, engaging in advocacy and social action so as to achieve societal conditions and structures that enhance family functioning, reaching for—and building on—the strengths and potentialities of parents and other family members, involving parents as partners in the helping process, and providing needed services and supports.

5. Children in care, biological families, foster families and other caregivers, social workers, court-appointed special advocates (CASAs), attorneys, parent aides, and other service providers constitute an ongoing partnership, promoted by effective teamwork. The differential roles of all parties should be clearly spelled out and understood.

6. Human diversity—for example, culture, race, ethnicity, ability—should be respected. Life-styles and child-rearing methods that might be considered different or unusual should be accepted so long as they promote a child's health and safety. This principle is especially crucial because a disproportionate number of children in care come from low-income families or families of color, whereas most practitioners are Caucasian and from the middle-class.

7. A commitment to early and consistent contact between the child and family is an essential ingredient in preparing for and maintaining a successful reunification. Child-family contact can serve as a laboratory in which both parties work on the problems that may have contributed to the need for placement and learn new ways to be together again.

8. Family reunification services should be offered for as long as they are needed to maintain the reconnection of a child with the family. For many families, intensive family reunification services may need to be followed by less intensive services. For a few families, some level of service may be necessary until the child is ready for independent living.

The Agency Context

The reunification of children and their families is more likely to be successful when an agency articulates its mission through a comprehensive framework of policies, practices, and resources. In particular, this involves the commitment of agency administrators to hiring social workers with a range of family reunification competencies, empowering them through appropriate decision-making authority and opportunities to further develop their skills, facilitating all aspects of service delivery, and continually seeking new directions and pursuing program improvements.

An agency context that supports family reunification practice needs to address numerous aspects in relation to agency policy, practice with children and families, collaboration with other systems, and staff development. Each of these areas is considered below; each reflects the definition, principles, and guidelines delineated in the preceding section.

Agency Policy

- In their work with the legal and judicial system, agency administrators and staff members are able to articulate clearly the concept of family reunification, particularly as it incorporates levels of family reunification.

- The agency assigns roles and tasks in a manner that ensures that practitioners helping to reunify children and families have adequate time and training to carry out the wide range of activities required for competent family reunification practice.

- Program funding is structured to ensure that resources are available to purchase services needed to effect and maintain reunification.

- The agency has clear guidelines for deciding when family reunification services will be purchased, as well as from whom. In addition, workers are given clear responsibilities with respect to obtaining, negotiating for, coordinating, and evaluating purchased services.

- The agency has mechanisms in place to ensure that practitioners can convey information about needed resources to program planners and decision makers.

- The continuing development and enhancement of the resources and supports needed for effective family reunification is an integral part of the agency's operations.

- The agency perceives and treats foster parents and other caregivers as team members in family reunification efforts.

- Helping caregivers, especially foster parents and their families, to prepare for separation from their foster children and deal with subsequent feelings of loss is a clearly identified aspect of the agency's family reunification practice.

- Agency policy contributes to a supportive work environment, one that empowers social workers through appropriate opportunities, rewards, reasonable workloads, and adequately allocated resources.

- The agency actively recruits staff members who reflect the racial and ethnic groups served by the agency.

- The agency uses supervision and consultation to enhance workers' skills and reinforce their learning.

- The agency has a system to evaluate, monitor, and promote its effectiveness in accomplishing family reunification.

- The agency allows adequate time following family reunification to provide needed services to families before their case must be closed. Moreover, the agency has practice guidelines for ensuring the family's access to services after case termination.

Practice with Children and Families

- The agency has a family-centered orientation.

- Every child in care is helped to make some type of connection with someone in his or her kinship network, regardless of the permanent plan for that child.

- The agency provides immediate, active, and ongoing support of visits between children and parents.

- The agency uses a uniform and integrated approach to assessment and case planning with all of the families it serves. Thus, the work on reunifying a family is directly related to the problems that caused the original family separation.

- The agency makes therapeutic use of placement in out-of-home care, using it as a vehicle for rehabilitation of the family as much as possible and for optimal reconnection of the child with the family.

- Before recommending to the court that a family be reunified, the agency holds a case staffing to ensure that all relevant sources of information have been consulted, guidelines for developing safety plans for children have been followed, and case goals have been achieved.

Collaboration with Other Systems

- To obtain the community supports needed by practitioners and the families they work with, the agency regularly convenes interdisciplinary, interagency teams for service planning.

- The agency maintains adequate linkage and collaboration with the judicial system and with legal personnel to ensure that the legal aspects of family reunification are facilitated.

- The agency works with the legislative system to develop statutory directives that support family reunification.

- To ensure that highly qualified and well-trained staff members are hired and retained, the agency maintains collaborative relationships with schools of social work, advising them on curriculum development and participating in educational activities.

Staff Development

- The agency provides regular in-service training in basic child welfare practice to its staff members, with attention to their varying levels of expertise.

5

- The agency's family reunification training builds on past training experiences and the expertise of each participating staff member.

- The agency regularly involves staff members in assessing training needs.

- The agency views foster parents and other caregivers as part of its service delivery team and regularly involves them in joint training with social workers.

- The agency's training activities model and seek to enhance partnerships and collaboration among caregivers, social workers, and service providers.

- The agency advocates for and participates in training in permanency planning for judges, attorneys, probation officers, guardians ad litem, and others who represent children and their families.

A Competency-Based Approach to Education and Training[2]

Competency-based, or performance-based, training is one of the most important developments in education for child welfare practice today. It consists of designing, delivering, and evaluating training that ties worker performance to the goals of an organization and its deployment of resources and comprises the following:

- a thorough job analysis that defines the knowledge, skills, and attitudes or values required of staff members throughout the agency;

- an accurate assessment of each person's individual learning needs, skills, and attitudes;

- a standardized curriculum that is based on a set of requisite knowledge, skills, and attitudes;

- a training delivery system that emphasizes the conditions that promote adult learning (particularly in being learner-centered rather than trainer-centered), takes different trainees' learning needs and styles into account, and has feedback mechanisms enabling staff members to monitor their own development and continue to learn and improve performance;

- an evaluation of learning outcomes in relation to both job performance *and* the achievement of agency goals and objectives; and

- a process for identifying obstacles to competent performance, such as workload, work environment, lack of resources, and policy limitations.

A competency-based approach has particular relevance for the specialized area of family reunification practice because it can tailor training to fit with what the provider needs to know to help families that have been separated. Thus, from a competency-based perspective, it is possible to identify what is new or different in family reunification as compared with other specialized areas of practice, such as family preservation. At the same time, this approach allows for identification of common knowledge and skills.

The educational materials on family reunification included in Part 3 of this volume are based on a set of knowledge, attitudes, and skills identified as necessary for successfully reunifying families. The materials address selected areas of competence, drawn from the full set of competencies outlined in Part 2. While these competencies are *specific* to family reunification practice, they build on generic or core—as well as specialized—child welfare competencies, in such areas as assessment, case planning, and the impact of separation and placement. Staff developers and educators interested in incorporating content on family reunification into their curricula by using a competency-based approach might wish to consult Part 2, in which the specialized knowledge, attitude, and skills needed for reunifying families are described.

Training is often selected as the first (and sometimes only) solution to improving child welfare programs. Isolated training events, however, and training that is not integral to all other aspects of a program, will not result in the desired outcomes: reunifying more children, more effectively and more quickly, with their families. A competency-based approach to training begins with setting standards for competence that aid in recruiting the best qualified staff. It also allows agencies to target training to the particular learning needs of staff members and thus increases the likelihood that the ability of staff members to reunify families successfully will improve. Moreover, a competency-based approach places the ability of staff members to work effectively within a broader context of agency supports needed to do the work.

Recurring Issues and Dilemmas

In the process of rethinking family reunification, it is also necessary to take into account recurring issues and dilemmas in child welfare. In family reunification practice, social workers, attorneys, judges, and others face a major challenge—deciding whether children, who have already been deemed to have been at a risk significant enough so as to necessitate their placement, *can* return home, and *when*.

This challenge raises a number of issues that must be taken into account in the development of policy, program, and practice in family reunification:

- How can we deal with the tension between the value of family preservation and the imperatives of child protection?

- What guidelines can help us assess the risk of returning children to their families versus the risk of prolonging their stay in out-of-home care?

- What is the minimum level of care and parenting that is adequate for family reunification? What constitutes "good enough" parenting?

- How can we implement the concept of levels of reconnection in practice? How will we know if a child and family have achieved their greatest level of reconnection? What does reconnection mean in contexts where parental rights are terminated and children are placed for adoption?

- Where do we draw the line between providing continuing supports to reunited families and perpetuating their dependence?

- How can providers apply reunification competencies differentially with different target populations (i.e., young children versus adolescents), or different settings (i.e., family foster care versus group or residential care)?

- How can we deal effectively with differences between the legal and social services systems, in relation to

such questions as whether, when, and how families should be reunified?

- How can we help families to function differently when their environments remain so harsh?

- How can we maintain or restore optimism and a belief in the potential of even the most challenging families to do what is best for their children, while also accepting that some parents cannot care for their children?

Attention to family reunification is but one expression of the renewed emphasis in child welfare and related fields on preserving families. The unique challenges of preserving families that have been separated through placement, however, require new thinking, informed policy changes, supportive programs, revised practice strategies, systematic attention to developing the competence of family reunification practitioners, collaboration among providers, and emphasis on hope and compassion.

Notes

1. A.N. Maluccio, R. Warsh, and B.A. Pine, "Family Reunification: An Overview," in *Together Again: Family Reunification in Foster Care*, edited by B.A. Pine, R. Warsh, and A.N. Maluccio (Washington, DC: Child Welfare League of America, 1993), p. 6.

2. Adapted from B.A. Pine, R. Warsh, and A.N. Maluccio, "Training for Competence in Family Reunification Practice," in *Together Again: Family Reunification in Foster Care*, edited by B.A. Pine, R. Warsh, and A.N. Maluccio (Washington, DC: Child Welfare League of America, 1993), pp. 33–50.

PART 2
Family Reunification Competencies
for Social Workers

- *Values and Attitudes*
- *Assessing Readiness for Family Reunification*
- *Goal Planning for Family Reunification*
- *Implementing the Family Reunification Plan*
- *Maintaining the Reunification and Ending the Service*

Family Reunification Competencies for Social Workers

Family reunification practice, following the definition and principles delineated in the first part of this book, requires a range of specialized competencies for social workers. These competencies are the basis for the training materials that appear later in this *Sourcebook*.

The practice competencies, which involve a set of knowledge, attitudes, and skills necessary for successfully reunifying families, are organized into five major parts, following the process of family reconnection after a child is placed out of the home: 1) practitioners commit themselves to a set of values and attitudes that guide their practice; 2) practitioners evaluate the family's readiness to reunify; 3) practitioners use the results of the assessment to formulate goals and service agreements; 4) practitioners work directly with children and parents and collaborate with other service providers; and 5) practitioners prepare the family to remain connected, end the service, and evaluate their work.

It should be noted that family reunification practice—like other forms of child welfare practice—is a dynamic process. Assessment, goal planning, implementation, and evaluation are interrelated practice activities that occur throughout work on a family reunification case. For example, social workers need to use their assessment skills when they plan case goals, their intervention skills when they help children cope with their feelings during the assessment phase, and their evaluation skills throughout the reunification process. The linear form reflected in this document is used only for purposes of conceptualization.

In addition, as already noted, it should be stressed that although these competencies are *specific* to family reunification practice, they build on generic or core, as well as specialized, child welfare competencies, in such areas as assessment, case planning, and the impact of separation and placement. Family reunification practice also requires practitioners to possess specialized competencies in related practice areas, such as family therapy, child abuse, and legal issues in child welfare. In short, the competent family reunification practitioner, whether serving families as a line worker in a public agency or as a

social worker in an intensive family-based program, is a specialist equipped with the full range of generic child welfare competencies* as well as the more specific competencies identified in this book.

Values and Attitudes

Social workers who are competent in family reunification practice:

1. Are guided by an ecologically-oriented, competence-centered perspective that stresses advocacy and social action to promote family preservation; identifying and mobilizing the strengths and potentials of children, parents, and families; understanding family functioning in the context of its environment; and providing social supports to families.

2. Appreciate and deal with their own experiences of separation and loss.

3. Value the biological family as the preferred child-rearing unit, believing that most families, if properly assisted, have the potential for positive change and can care for their children.

4. View family reunification as a process with a continuum of outcomes or goals for reunification services—from full reentry into the family system to other, less intense forms of contact that may be optimal for some children and families.

5. Recognize the wide range of symbols of family membership, such as family photo albums, letters, birth certificates, and other documents that can be used to support and promote a child's kinship bonds.

6. Recognize the importance to some children in care of primary caretakers other than the biological parents, including adoptive parents, grandparents, and other members of the extended kinship system.

---

*   Selected references on generic competencies in child welfare as well as competency-based training may be found in Part 4, Selected References. See especially Hughes and Rycus [1989].

7. Are committed to family reunification efforts that respect family integrity and promote empowerment of children and families.

8. Examine and deal with their own beliefs, feelings, values, and attitudes in relation to parenting and to reunifying families, identifying in particular those that may serve as obstacles to reunification.

9. Convey to the child, family, foster parents, and others, as early as possible in a child's out-of-home placement, their own and the agency's commitment to working diligently to return the child home or pursuing other more appropriate forms of connectedness to the family.

10. Value diversity of family styles, life-styles, and child-rearing methods so long as they promote a child's health and safety.

11. See early and consistent family contact as an essential ingredient in preparing for and maintaining a successful reunification.

12. Recognize that family reunification practice requires the services of numerous systems—legal, health, mental health, and education—and thus realize the importance of collaboration and advocacy in behalf of families.

13. Appreciate that family reunification services should be offered for as long as they are needed to maintain the reconnection.

Assessing Readiness for Family Reunification

Social workers who are competent in family reunification practice:

1. Enter the biological and foster family systems in a manner that promotes trust and confidence, recognizing in particular the range of feelings family members may experience in conjunction with reunification efforts, including feelings resulting from the experience of separation and the type of placement (i.e., anger, frustration, fear, resentment, shame, grief).

2. Begin to assess readiness for family reunification as early as possible in the course of a child's placement in out-of-home care.

3. Use the process of joining with the family as a way to assess family rules, patterns, power structure, and functioning.

4. Use assessment approaches that are congruent with the family's heritage, recognizing the ways in which cultural variables can affect an assessment.

5. Identify those individuals beyond the immediate family whose involvement in the reunification effort is essential (i.e., extended family, clergy).

6. Appreciate the impact of the placement in out-of-home care on the child, parents, and other family members, as well as the impact of feelings of loss and separation.

7. Conduct, when necessary, a search for parents and other family members whose whereabouts are unknown.

8. Assess the child's and family's functioning and situation, especially in relation to:

   • the family's willingness and readiness to be reunited with the child and the child's willingness and readiness to reconnect with the family;

   • the parent's ability to meet the physical, social, emotional, medical, and educational needs of the child;

   • the impact on the child and family of experiences with child abuse and sexual abuse;

   • the child's functioning and special needs;

   • the family relationships, level of parent/child bonding, family communication patterns, family conflict resolution skills, children's relationships, and parental functioning;

   • the strengths, resources, and potentialities of the parents and child that can make reunion possible, with special appreciation of the strengths and resources in families whose life-styles, family styles, and child-rearing methods differ from one's own;

   • the formal and informal resources and supports available to the family through its extended kin networks and the social service and community systems;

   • the family problems (i.e., substance abuse, domestic violence, poverty, homelessness, mental illness, parents' inability to put child's needs above their own) that may impede reunification or suggest consideration of forms of reconnection other than reunion;

   • the relationships between parents and foster parents or child care workers and other service providers that promote or impede reunification.

9. Identify environmental obstacles and other threats to reunification, including resource gaps, attitudes and values of practitioners and others, inadequate policies and legal procedures, service needs, lack of community resources, and other outside pressures and stresses.

10. When return home is not possible, identify an optimal degree of reconnection that the family and child can be helped to establish or reestablish and maintain.

11. Weigh the risk of reunification against the risk of continued placement.

12. Evaluate the family's and child's progress toward reunification on an ongoing basis.

Goal Planning for Family Reunification

Social workers who are competent in family reunification practice:

1. Understand that goal planning is both a product and a process that:

   * requires explanation so parents and children understand its purpose;

   * involves the child and family in mutual decision making;

   * occurs throughout work with a family up to case closure; and

   * requires continual monitoring, reassessment, and revision.

2. Help the children, parents, and other family members form a partnership that works to establish agreed-upon goals.

3. Obtain and share with the child and family information about their history to help them understand the past and prepare for the future.

4. Plan to help children, parents, and other family members cope with their feelings about—and reactions to—the experience of loss and separation.

5. Work with the family to identify the optimal level of reconnection that is possible—from actual reunification of the child with the family to visiting or other forms of contact—recognizing that both the plan

and the timeline for achieving it need to be somewhat flexible.

6. Explain to family members, children, and others as appropriate why the child is being reunited with the family, including reasons for original placement, what has changed or needs to change to make reunification possible, what is involved in the process of family reunification, and why the particular level of reconnection is being sought.

7. Work with family members to help them develop and prioritize the goals that must be reached in order to effect a reunification. Goals should be specific, attainable, and clearly stated, preferably using the family's words or words that are most meaningful to them, with emphasis on behavioral changes that are directly related to the reasons the child was removed.

8. Take into account laws and policies that affect reunification, incorporating the requirements of the legal system into goal planning with the family and helping to ensure that the court's decision-making process is in concert with professional recommendations.

9. Work with the parents, the child, and the foster parents and other service providers to develop a service agreement for implementing the plan. The agreement should spell out the roles and tasks of all participants and be directly related to the original reasons for the child's removal. In particular, the service agreement should include:

   * a rationale, goals, and expectations;

   * the roles each party will play in achieving the plan;

   * the tasks each party must complete to provide for the child's growth, health, and safety, and the family's integrity;

   * small, concrete tasks that can be readily achieved;

   * a visiting plan that addresses ways to work on parent-child relationship issues identified in the assessment;

   * a timetable, including a target date for return home or other form of family reconnection, that best reflects a child's and family's pace for goal attainment;

   * a plan for the child's transition to another school system, if necessary;

- a plan for supporting the child, parents, and family following the reunion and after case closure; and

- any support parents might need to achieve their goals (i.e., transportation).

10. Support children, parents, and other family members as they are involved in decision making regarding family reunification.

11. Regularly convene formal and informal reviews of progress toward the goals delineated in the service agreement, revising or amending the goals as needed. Such reviews should be planned and implemented with the active involvement of family members, caregivers, and service providers, *and* with recognition that parents often feel intimidated and overwhelmed by a group of experts and may not feel free to express their own opinions.

Implementing the Family Reunification Plan

Social workers who are competent in family reunification practice:

1. Work directly with the children, parents, and other family members to prepare them for the desired form of family reunification by:

- developing a child's placement diary, with parents if possible, reflecting significant events that occurred during the placement in out-of-home care and including important documents that families would want to have;

- demonstrating respect for diversity in life-styles, family systems, and child-rearing approaches;

- helping them cope with the range of feelings that may be experienced when preparing for reunification (i.e., ambivalence, unrealistically high or low expectations, the impact of loss and separation) and recognizing that a child's return to the family is like a new placement, inasmuch as the child and family may have changed;

- working on issues of family functioning that led to the need for placement, using, where appropriate, conjoint sessions with parents, siblings, child, and other significant family members;

- practicing with the family, at the time of reunification, ways of handling a recurrence of problems.

2. Work specifically with the parents by:

- helping them identify and accept the ways in which they and their children have changed while they were apart;

- helping other children in the family cope with changes brought on by reunification;

- identifying those behaviors they might expect to see in their children following reconnection;

- helping them to learn the positive parenting skills necessary for achieving the particular level of reconnection, especially in relation to:

  - arranging for their child's access to adequate food, clothing, housing, health care, and education;

  - recognizing and appreciating their child's achievements;

  - identifying and responding appropriately to their child's problem areas;

  - providing discipline in a constructive way;

  - giving emotional nurturance to their child;

  - using and interacting with community resources in behalf of their child;

  - helping their child feel positively about him/herself and other family members;

  - sharing family and cultural values; and

  - teaching about cultural rituals and celebrations.

- helping them communicate with court personnel.

- focusing on preparing them for reunification by:

  - helping them understand and prepare for their child's feelings toward the foster parents;

  - relating the plan for improving parenting skills (as noted above) to the selected family reunification goal, recognizing, for example, that a family that will reconnect by visiting on the telephone needs different skills from one that will reconnect by living together; and

  - engaging in a realistic assessment of their progress toward service goals.

3. Work specifically with the child by:

- helping the child deal with a sense of divided loyalty toward biological and foster families;

- providing opportunities for the child to learn coping skills and positive behaviors for family reunification;

- using developmentally appropriate methods—role playing, puppet shows, storytelling—to explain the reunification, including reasons for original placement, what has already or still needs to be changed to make reconnection possible, and what steps come next;

- helping the child cope with feelings that may be reactivated as departure from the foster family approaches, such as loss, guilt, anger, and grief; and

- helping the child to communicate with various court personnel.

4. Use visiting to prepare for reunification by:

- recognizing the conditions that optimize positive visiting and using them to bring about a positive contact, including selecting a site and planning and structuring visiting in such a way that parents' caregiving skills are enhanced;

- arranging visiting along a continuum of increasingly stressful times (i.e., playing in the park to mealtimes to difficult bedtimes) in order to help parents gradually achieve competence in these areas;

- planning and conducting a pre-visit briefing and review of the visiting experience with each of the parties involved, including foster parents;

- recognizing the full range of activities that constitute visiting, such as clothes shopping, class trips, and pediatric appointments;

- recognizing and overcoming those obstacles that make visiting difficult for children, parents, and other family members;

- providing assistance with the travel arrangements for visiting between the child, parents, or other family members;

- recognizing the importance of and arranging for sibling contacts (i.e., sleepovers, vacations, therapy);

- progressively increasing the length of visits and parental responsibilities;

- documenting visiting experiences to support recommendations pertaining to reunification; and

- evaluating and altering the visiting plan in accordance with the family's and child's progress and needs.

5. Promote the foster family's collaboration and participation in family reunification by:

- facilitating collaboration and communication between foster parents and biological parents, including clarifying and negotiating the respective or complementary roles of biological parents and foster parents;

- accepting and implementing the concept of foster parents as professionals, as members of the service team, and as partners in service delivery;

- helping foster parents to serve as resources to the biological family, capable of providing new skills, knowledge, and empathy, by giving them sufficient information about the child and family to understand their role with a particular family;

- helping foster parents to identify and build on the biological family's strengths; and

- conveying to the foster parents the importance of their giving the child "permission" to reconnect with the biological family.

6. Collaborate with other service providers by:

- facilitating teamwork among them;

- working closely with the child's school;

- advocating for appropriate legal statutes and policies that support family reunification;

- negotiating with service providers in behalf of families and advocating for a wide range of needed services, and evaluating the effectiveness of services provided;

- helping parents to attain skills in working in their own behalf with service providers and the education, health, and legal systems;

- identifying and carrying out the range of tasks related to legally reconnecting the child and family, including preparing and giving court testimony; and

- working with the legal and court systems to facilitate implementation of the reunification plan.

7. Maintain accurate and complete records of service activities and child and family progress, and use these

records appropriately to determine the attainment of case goals.

Maintaining the Reunification and Ending the Service

Social workers who are competent in family reunification practice:

1. Prepare family members to remain connected with one another by:

   • enabling them to recognize the strengths in themselves and the supports in their community that can help maintain the family;

   • planning with them ways to handle problems as they arise;

   • helping them to recognize that problems will occur—they do in all families—and that problems do not signal failure;

   • helping them to form or strengthen linkages with formal and informal social supports;

   • helping them to work through their feelings about the social worker's impending departure.

2. Engage foster parents in the post-reunification phase by:

   • helping foster family members cope with their feelings regarding the child's reunification;

   • reinforcing feelings of security within the family for the "other" children in light of the separations and reunions (i.e., biological children of the foster parents and other foster children in the home);

   • identifying when a foster family, whose foster child has returned home, has worked through their feelings and is ready to accept another foster child; and

   • helping the biological family and foster parents to clarify their relationship following reunification (i.e., foster parents' willingness to provide respite, availability for phone contact or visits).

3. Deal effectively with the disruption of a reunification plan by:

   • using the disruption to learn more about a child and parents in order to make another permanent plan;

   • reassessing the optimal level of continuing connection between child and family following the disruption;

   • recognizing that disruption in some cases may be a temporary setback and not necessarily a failure; and

   • dealing with the reality of disruption of reconnected families by helping family members and children to cope with their feelings while effectively managing their own possible feelings of failure.

4. Hold a closing session with the family and others to summarize accomplishments, elaborate on family strengths, prioritize the work that remains, and review the supports that can help the family carry out the tasks ahead.

5. Build on their experiences with each case by:

   • assessing and analyzing what was learned, particularly in relation to their own practice as well as the agency's services;

   • evaluating program implementation as well as impact (not just whether it worked, but how the way in which the reunion was implemented influenced the outcome of the reunion plan); and

   • disseminating what is learned, ultimately influencing agency policy and practice.

PART 3
Curriculum Modules for
Teaching Family Reunification

- *Using the Curriculum*
- *Curriculum Module I: Redefining Family Reunification*
- *Curriculum Module II: Differing Perspectives on Family Reunification*
- *Curriculum Module III: Developing Policy and Program in Family Reunification*
- *Curriculum Module IV: Visiting—The Heart of Family Reunification*
- *Curriculum Module V: Learning from a Case Study*

The five modules in this curriculum are for use by trainers and educators in child welfare agencies, schools of social work, and other training programs for practitioners, administrators, foster parents, or child care workers. They are intended to influence values about, as well as increase knowledge and skills in, family reunification.

For training delivered in child welfare agencies, the modules may be used individually as part of the agency's orientation program, or the set of five may be incorporated into a more comprehensive training plan. In undergraduate or graduate schools of social work, the modules can also be used individually, as learning resources for courses, including those on direct practice, research, policy, and administration, or they can be adapted for specialized courses in family and children's services according to the requirements and needs of a particular school. They may also be adapted for other service providers, including legal and court personnel. As such, they can be used in schools of law and in continuing education programs for attorneys and judges. In adapting the modules, each instructor should develop learning outcomes based on the specific learning needs of the participants and the objectives of the educational program.

Module Content

Each of the first four modules includes 1) a statement of purpose; 2) the suggested audience; 3) key teaching points, key content areas, and notes for the instructor; 4) a list of handouts needed (handouts for each module, in a form suitable for photocopying, appear at the end of each module); 5) directions and suggestions for learning activities; and 6) references. Module V contains a comprehensive set of discussion questions that reinforce and build on the content covered in the previous modules.

Modules I through III have been designed for two- to three-hour sessions and may easily be adapted for either classroom or workshop use. While each module can stand alone, because they are interrelated, it is recommended that instructors use as many as time and the objectives of the educational program permit.

Module IV on family visiting requires about eight hours to complete. It contains five units—an introductory unit, three units designed around the phases of placement (the initial, middle, and transitioning phases), and a brief unit demonstrating how, using a competency-based approach, participants can evaluate their learning and develop plans for applying new knowledge and skills to their practice. Greater emphasis is placed on visiting than on other areas because it is such a key part of family reunification practice and a highly influential factor in the outcome of family reunification efforts. The emphasis on visiting provides participants with an intensive opportunity to learn and/or enhance the specialized attitudes, knowledge, and skills required for competent family reunification practice. The material contained in Module IV, as indicated earlier, draws from the work of Peg McCartt Hess, Kathleen Ohman Proch, Gail Folaron, and Edith Fein.

Module V includes a detailed case study, developed by Vincent E. Faherty, of a child welfare agency's attempts to reunite a family separated by the placement of its children in family foster care. Because of the extensive publicity that surrounded this case, the study provides a rich source of data to illustrate various aspects of policy, program, and practice in family reunification, particularly those that are most troubling and in need of attention. Discussion questions and learning activities in this capstone module highlight the themes brought out in Modules I through IV.

Module I

REDEFINING FAMILY REUNIFICATION

REDEFINING FAMILY REUNIFICATION

Time	Two hours
Purpose	This module introduces a new way of thinking about family reunification. It helps practitioners make the shift from a narrow and more traditional view of reunification— a child's return home to live with his or her family—to a broader one that encompasses the concept of *levels of reconnection*—that is, viewing family reunification as a continuum, with levels of reconnection ranging from living together to other forms of contact, such as visiting. Using a case example, participants will consider the policy, practice, and programmatic implications of this concept.
Suggested Audience	Social workers, administrators, foster parents, parent aides, child care workers, attorneys, and judges
Handouts Needed	Handout I–1: A Definition of Family Reunification
	Handout I–2: Underlying Principles and Guidelines for Family Reunification
	Handout I–3: Case Example—The Green Family

Key Teaching Points

1. The expanded definition ...

   - assumes that family reunification is an integral part of the philosophy and practice of family preservation and permanency planning, with their emphasis on ensuring continuity of care for children;

   - views family reunification as a continuum, with levels or outcomes ranging from full reentry into the family system to partial reentry to less extensive contact such as visiting, phoning, writing, and other affirmations of the child's membership in the family;

   - underscores the value of maintaining and enhancing connectedness or reconnectedness between children in out-of-home care and their families; and

   - recognizes that not every parent can be a daily caregiver and that some families, though not able to live together, can still maintain kinship bonds.

2. It is important to think about family reunification in a broad and flexible way because:

   - even when parents cannot assume daily care of their children, they have an important role to play as family members;

   - most families can be helped to identify and maintain a level of reconnection that preserves kinship bonds;

   - kinship bonds are essential to a child's development of a healthy sense of self;

   - children form important kinship ties to significant others such as grandparents, godparents, foster parents, and adoptive parents;

   - where children live can and should be considered separately from the importance of family membership and its maintenance;

- family membership and kinship ties are key to successful permanency planning for children;

- family reunification is a dynamic process, not a one-time event (i.e., move back home);

- individual needs must be identified and met in a wide range of circumstances; and

- service providers must be encouraged to think more hopefully about families.

3. Family reunification practice needs to be supported by agency policies that promote family empowerment and integrity, thus enabling families to build on their strengths, while working to meet their needs.

4. Related systems, such as the judicial and mental health systems, need to establish and carry out policies that support the concept of levels of family reunification.

Directions

1. Before presenting the more expanded definition included with this module, ask participants to share their views on what family reunification means to them. Note key ideas and themes on a flip chart or on newsprint taped to the wall.

2. Distribute *Handout I–1: A Definition of Family Reunification* and *Handout I–2: Underlying Principles and Guidelines for Family Reunification*. Review them with participants.

3. As a group, discuss the following questions related to the new definition:

- How is this definition similar to/different from your own concept of family reunification?

- What is your agency's and/or the court's explicit or implicit definition of family reunification?

- What are the implications for policy and/or practice of such an expanded definition?

- What is meant by the concept of *levels of reconnection*? Does anyone have examples of this concept from their experience with families?

4. Have participants read a case example in which a child and family have been separated by placement. *Handout I–3: Case Example—The Green Family* may be used, or participants may use a case example from their own practice.

5. As a group, discuss the following questions related to the concept of levels of reconnection:

- How is the potential for the child and family to maintain a relationship influenced by considering other forms of reconnection beyond return home?

- What optimal level of reconnection might the child and family be helped to identify and achieve?

- What family strengths would you identify and build on to support this goal? What needs would have to be met?

- How do you think visiting should be used to achieve reconnection in this case?

- How can the child's foster parents best support implementation of this concept?

- What are the possible risks to the child if the identified level of reconnection is sought?

6. Ask participants to consider the policy and program implications of this concept.

- What policies and programs would agencies need to develop to promote such practice?

- How could the court system be helped to recognize and act on this concept?

References

Maluccio, A.N.; Warsh, R.; and Pine, B.A. "Family Reunification: An Overview." In *Together Again: Family Reunification in Foster Care*, edited by B.A. Pine, R. Warsh, and A.N. Maluccio. Washington, DC: Child Welfare League of America, 1993, pp. 3–19.

Zamosky, J.; Sparks, J.; Hatt, R.; and Sharman, J. "Believing in Families." In *Together Again: Family Reunification in Foster Care*, edited by B.A. Pine, R. Warsh, and A.N. Maluccio. Washington, DC: Child Welfare League of America, 1993, pp. 155–175.

A DEFINITION OF FAMILY REUNIFICATION*

Family reunification is the planned process of reconnecting children in out-of-home care with their families by means of a variety of services and supports to the children, their families, and their foster parents or other service providers. It aims to help each child and family to achieve and maintain, at any given time, their optimal level of reconnection—from full reentry of the child into the family system to other forms of contact, such as visiting, that affirm the child's membership in the family.

---

* From A.N. Maluccio, R. Warsh, and B.A. Pine, "Family Reunification: An Overview," in *Together Again: Family Reunification in Foster Care*, edited by B.A. Pine, R. Warsh, and A.N. Maluccio (Washington, DC: Child Welfare League of America, 1993), p. 6.

UNDERLYING PRINCIPLES AND GUIDELINES
FOR FAMILY REUNIFICATION

1. Family reunification is an integral part of the philosophy of preserving families and of permanency planning, with their emphasis on ensuring continuity of care for children. Family reunification should be systematically considered and planned for by the child welfare and legal systems as early as possible in a child's placement in out-of-home care.

2. Family reunification is a dynamic process that must be based on the child's and family's changing qualities, needs, and potentialities. It should be viewed as a continuum, with levels or outcomes ranging from full reentry into the family system to partial reentry to less extensive contact. At any point during the child's placement in out-of-home care, the most appropriate or optimal level of reconnection should be identified and actively pursued. At the same time, it should be recognized that reconnection is not possible or desirable in some situations, and that those situations may appropriately require termination of parental rights. Even in such instances, however, children should at the least be helped to move into new permanent families with some tangible tie to their past in the form of pictures, a lifebook, or other family memorabilia.

3. As a form of preserving families, reunification embodies (a) conviction about the role of the biological family as the preferred child-rearing unit, if at all possible; (b) recognition of the potential of most families to care for their children, if properly assisted; (c) awareness of the impact of separation and loss on children and parents; and (d) involvement, as appropriate, of any and all members of the child's family, including members of the extended family who, while not legally related, are considered by the child and themselves to be "family."

4. Reunification practice is guided by an ecologically oriented, competence-centered perspective that emphasizes promoting family empowerment, engaging in advocacy and social action so as to achieve societal conditions and structures that enhance family functioning; reaching for—and building on—the strengths and potentialities of parents and other family members, involving parents as partners in the helping process; and providing needed services and supports.

5. Children in care, biological families, foster families and other caregivers, social workers, court-appointed special advocates (CASAs), attorneys, parent aides, and other service providers should constitute an ongoing partnership, promoted by effective teamwork. The differential roles of all parties should be clearly spelled out and understood.

6. Human diversity—for example, culture, race, ethnicity, ability—should be respected. Life-styles and child-rearing methods that might be considered different or unusual should be accepted so long as they promote a child's health and safety. This principle is especially crucial because a disproportionate number of children in care come from low-income families or families of color, whereas most practitioners are Caucasian and from the middle-class.

7. A commitment to early and consistent contact between the child and family is an essential ingredient in preparing for and maintaining a successful reunification. Child-family contact can serve as a laboratory in which both parties work on the problems that may have contributed to the need for placement and learn new ways to be together again.

8. Family reunification services should be offered for as long as they are needed to maintain the reconnection of a child with the family. For many families, intensive family reunification services may need to be followed by less intensive services. For a few families, some level of service may be necessary until the child is ready for independent living.

CASE EXAMPLE—
THE GREEN FAMILY*

Participants

- Andy Green, age five. Voluntarily placed in out-of-home care by his mother when he was three.

- Julie Green, Andy's mother. Grew up in foster care. Has no family support.

- Jack Green, Andy's father.

- Paul Lawson, Julie Green's live-in boyfriend.

History

Andy has been diagnosed as having an attention deficit disorder and is on Ritalin. He suffers from seizures and is known to walk in his sleep. He has destroyed stuffed animals, started fires, demonstrated acts of self-mutilation and at one point drank a bottle of Tylenol. There is concern that Andy has been physically, sexually, and emotionally abused, and emotionally neglected.

Andy has been placed in three different family foster homes. The first move was at the foster parent's request because of Andy's behavior; the second move was the result of physical abuse by the foster parent and sexual abuse by a foster brother. He has been in his current foster home for seven months. His foster mother asks for a lot of emotional support to cope with Andy's difficult behavior, but remains committed to caring for him. Andy appears to like her, but says he doesn't think anyone wants him. He has expressed an interest in living with his father.

Ms. Green is overwhelmed by Andy's behavior and her interest in Andy can best be described as ambivalent. She has visited irregularly and missed many scheduled appointments. She has, however, followed through on plans to phone Andy, and both report that they look forward to their times on the phone.

Andy's father expressed an interest in Andy but is frequently inconsistent in following through with agency requests. He visits less than offered, was slow to establish paternity as ordered, and failed to follow through with a psychological evaluation. Mr. Green has a history of substance abuse and, according to Ms. Green, has a tendency to become physically abusive. Ms. Green states that he seriously injured her back in their last confrontation.

Ms. Green describes Paul Lawson, with whom she has a relationship, as her live-in boyfriend. Ms. Green admitted that there were some problems between Mr. Lawson and Andy. Mr. Lawson is "extremely short tempered" and Ms. Green is afraid he may seriously hurt Andy. Ms. Green said she would sign papers for an open adoption, but believes that will terminate her parental rights, giving Mr. Green the decision-making power over Andy.

Ms. Green believes that institutions should be established for young children so that they can have one place to live—a place where they can stay and won't have to move. In terms of placement in her own home, Ms. Green says, "I'd have to make a choice if they decided to return Andy. I'd have to choose Andy, of course, because he is my child. But I don't know. So I'm not making any choices."

* The authors are grateful to Peg McCartt Hess, Columbia University School of Social Work, and Gail Folaron, Indiana University School of Social Work, who provided the material on which this case example is based.

Module II

DIFFERING PERSPECTIVES ON FAMILY REUNIFICATION

DIFFERING PERSPECTIVES ON FAMILY REUNIFICATION

Time	Two hours
Purpose	Family reunification typically requires participation by several professionals, whose different values, ideas, and recommendations may clash. This module will increase participants' awareness of the views, issues, and challenges inherent in family reunification from such perspectives as those of the biological parent, foster parent, social worker, parent aide, judge, and child welfare agency administrator. The module is set up as a roundtable discussion by participants who are willing to assume these functions in a role-play or who actually function in these capacities.*
Suggested Audience	Social workers, administrators, foster parents, parent aides, child care workers, attorneys, and judges
Handout Needed	Handout II–1: Case Example—The Green Family

Key Teaching Points

1. Extensive collaboration and teamwork are required in family reunification practice—teamwork involving the child, parents and other family members, foster parents, teachers, social workers, parent aides, legal and judicial personnel, and other service providers.

2. It is easy to get discouraged in many case situations involving family reunification. For example, the written word in case summaries, agency referrals, or court records often conditions us to think or feel that it will not be possible to get a particular family together again. It is therefore critical to avoid being overly influenced by the written word, to get to know parents as human beings, and to join with parents in an exploration of their situations and possible solutions or options.

3. Collaboration should be the hallmark of service provision—from assessment, through case planning and implementation, to evaluation and follow-up. The role of foster parents in each phase of the helping process should be especially prominent.

4. Assessment needs to be comprehensive, involve all parties, and give special attention to the perspectives of the child, parents, and other family members.

5. Services should be provided not only on a comprehensive basis, but also in a way that avoids fragmentation (such as dealing with *either* the child *or* the parents), emphasizes a family system orientation, and views the family as the focus of attention.

6. Some families need help on a long-term basis, beyond the time limit typical of various intensive family preservation models. Long-term changes in families often require continued supports or services, to build on or enhance the gains made through intensive, time-limited family preservation services.

7. Further attention should be given to the roles and functions of other systems interfacing with child welfare, particularly the education, health, and mental health systems.

---

* For an expanded session, the instructor may want to use the panel format described here with the case material on the Cooper Family in Module V.

8. There may be conflict between the professional processes of assessment and case planning, and the value of family empowerment. Involving parents as partners in the helping process, therefore, requires deliberate and persistent efforts on the part of practitioners.

9. There is a need to recognize obstacles to effective reunification practice, and to develop strategies for overcoming them. Obstacles may take the form of limited funding and other resources; territorial disputes among service providers; inadequate interagency and interdisciplinary collaboration; insufficient training for foster parents, social workers, parent aides, court personnel, and other service providers; and turnover among judicial, legal, and social work personnel.

10. The many parties involved in family reunification have very different needs, interests, and goals. What is important is understanding and dealing effectively with these differences.

Directions*

1. In advance of the session, select a moderator for the roundtable. The instructor may want to play this role or invite a participant to do so. In addition, select the panelists: biological parent, foster parent, social worker, parent aide, judge, and child welfare agency administrator. Ideally, it would be helpful to have actual representatives of each of the above to participate in the forum. If this is not feasible, course participants can be asked to play the roles.

3. Ask the panelists to read a case summary in advance. You may use *Handout II–1: Case Example—The Green Family* or any other case, but participants should be familiar with it in advance. Panelists should come to the roundtable prepared to discuss the following issues:

   • As the (biological parent, foster parent, social worker, parent aide, judge, or agency administrator) in this case, what do you see as your primary obligation?

   • What are the main goals that you see in this case, particularly in relation to family reunification?

   • What do you think is the biggest challenge this case presents in relation to family reunification?

   • What would you need from the other people around this table as you attempted to reach case goals?

   • What are, or could be, obstacles to meeting case goals?

   • How would you change policy and/or programs to improve the family's chances of being reunified?

4. Following a brief introduction by each panelist of her or his connection with family reunification (i.e., "as a judge, my role in relation to reunifying children and their families is to…"), the moderator should ask each to discuss her or his perspective on family reunification in relation to the case example used and the questions posed above. The emphasis should be on a spontaneous flow of conversation in response to the above points.

5. The moderator should invite participants to question the panel members or express their views on the issues that emerge.

6. The moderator should pull together the key themes (teaching points) that emerge from the panel discussion and audience participation.

References

Day, P.; Cahn, K.; and Johnson, P. "Building Court-Agency Partnerships to Reunify Families." In *Together Again: Family Reunification in Foster Care*, edited by B.A. Pine, R. Warsh, and A.N. Maluccio. Washington, DC: Child Welfare League of America, 1993, pp. 21–34.

Boutilier, L., and Rehm, D. "Family Reunification Practice in a Community-Based Mental Health Center." In *Together Again: Family Reunification in Foster Care*, edited by B.A. Pine, R. Warsh, and A.N. Maluccio. Washington, DC: Child Welfare League of America, 1993, pp. 51–64.

---

* If this module is to be used with participants in conjunction with Module III, panelists' perspectives and audience suggestions for changing policies and programs can be recorded on newsprint for later use.

CASE EXAMPLE—
THE GREEN FAMILY*

Participants

- Andy Green, age five. Voluntarily placed in out-of-home care by his mother when he was three.

- Julie Green, Andy's mother. Grew up in foster care. Has no family support.

- Jack Green, Andy's father.

- Paul Lawson, Julie Green's live-in boyfriend.

History

Andy has been diagnosed as having an attention deficit disorder and is on Ritalin. He suffers from seizures and is known to walk in his sleep. He has destroyed stuffed animals, started fires, demonstrated acts of self-mutilation and at one point drank a bottle of Tylenol. There is concern that Andy has been physically, sexually, and emotionally abused, and emotionally neglected.

Andy has been placed in three different family foster homes. The first move was at the foster parent's request because of Andy's behavior; the second move was the result of physical abuse by the foster parent and sexual abuse by a foster brother. He has been in his current foster home for seven months. His foster mother asks for a lot of emotional support to cope with Andy's difficult behavior, but remains committed to caring for him. Andy appears to like her, but says he doesn't think anyone wants him. He has expressed an interest in living with his father.

Ms. Green is overwhelmed by Andy's behavior and her interest in Andy can best be described as ambivalent. She has visited irregularly and missed many scheduled appointments. She has, however, followed through on plans to phone Andy, and both report that they look forward to their times on the phone.

Andy's father expressed an interest in Andy but is frequently inconsistent in following through with agency requests. He visits less than offered, was slow to establish paternity as ordered, and failed to follow through with a psychological evaluation. Mr. Green has a history of substance abuse and, according to Ms. Green, has a tendency to become physically abusive. Ms. Green states that he seriously injured her back in their last confrontation.

Ms. Green describes Paul Lawson, with whom she has a relationship, as her live-in boyfriend. Ms. Green admitted that there were some problems between Mr. Lawson and Andy. Mr. Lawson is "extremely short tempered" and Ms. Green is afraid he may seriously hurt Andy. Ms. Green said she would sign papers for an open adoption, but believes that will terminate her parental rights, giving Mr. Green the decision-making power over Andy.

Ms. Green believes that institutions should be established for young children so that they can have one place to live—a place where they can stay and won't have to move. In terms of placement in her own home, Ms. Green says, "I'd have to make a choice if they decided to return Andy. I'd have to choose Andy, of course, because he is my child. But I don't know. So I'm not making any choices."

* The authors are grateful to Peg McCartt Hess, Columbia University School of Social Work, and Gail Folaron, Indiana University School of Social Work, who provided the material on which this case example is based.

Module III

DEVELOPING POLICY AND PROGRAM
IN FAMILY REUNIFICATION

DEVELOPING POLICY AND PROGRAM
IN FAMILY REUNIFICATION

Time	Two hours
Purpose	This module is designed to sensitize participants to a set of premises in family reunification practice and to involve them in developing a program model of agency policy and practice based on these premises. The module could also be used with agency administrators, supervisors, or policy makers in child welfare; for example, the exercise could serve as the basis for a more extensive program planning effort including development of an action plan to enhance the agency's family reunification efforts.
Suggested Audience	Social workers, administrators, foster parents, and parent aides
Handouts Needed	Handout III–1: A Definition of Family Reunification
	Handout III–2: Underlying Principles and Guidelines for Family Reunification
	Handout III–3: Building a Framework for a Family Reunification Program

Key Teaching Points

The list below highlights selected policy, program, and practice characteristics of a model family reunification program.

Policy and Program

1. The unique opportunities available to caregivers for assisting families to be reunited are recognized and used to the fullest extent. This includes caregivers' roles as resources to families following reunification and closing of the case.

2. Roles and tasks are assigned in such a way that practitioners helping to reunify children and families have adequate time and training to carry out the wide range of activities required for competent family reunification practice.

3. Program funding is structured so as to ensure that resources are available to purchase services needed to effect and maintain reunification.

4. The agency has clear guidelines for deciding when family reunification services will be purchased, as well as from whom. In addition, workers are given clear responsibilities with respect to obtaining, negotiating with, coordinating, and evaluating purchased services.

5. The agency has instituted a mechanism to ensure that practitioners can convey information about needed resources to policymakers, program planners, and decision makers.

6. The continuing development and enhancement of resources and supports needed for effective family reunification is an integral part of the agency's operations.

7. Foster parents and other caregivers are viewed and treated as team members in family reunification efforts.

8. Helping caregivers, especially foster parents and their families, to prepare for separation from their foster children and deal with subsequent feelings of loss is a clearly identified aspect of family reunification practice.

9. Agency policy contributes to a supportive work environment, one that empowers social workers through appropriate opportunities and rewards, reasonable workloads, and adequate allocation of resources.

10. There is active recruitment of staff members who reflect the racial and ethnic groups served by the agency.

11. Supervision and consultation are used to enhance workers' skills and reinforce their learning.

12. There is a system of evaluation to monitor and promote the agency's effectiveness in accomplishing family reunification.

13. Agency policy is written so as to ensure adequate time following family reunification to provide needed services to families before their cases must be closed. Moreover, the agency has practice guidelines for ensuring the family's access to services after case termination.

14. The agency takes a uniform and integrated approach to assessment and case planning with all of the families it serves. Thus, the work on reunifying a family is directly related to the problems that caused the original family separation.

15. Therapeutic use is made of placement in out-of-home care, both as a vehicle for rehabilitation of the family as much as possible, and as a means of achieving optimal reconnection of the child with the family.

16. Agency staff receive specialized family reunification training, including legal training, so that they might better serve families in a variety of ways, such as advocating for parental involvement in decision making.

17. Foster parents receive specialized training to enhance their role in relation to family reunification.

18. Interdisciplinary collaboration is fostered by conducting training sessions that bring together the full range of service providers to develop a common vision and language, and goals consistent with competent family reunification practice.

19. To obtain the community supports needed by practitioners and the families they work with, the agency regularly convenes interdisciplinary, interagency teams for service planning.

20. There is adequate linkage and collaboration with the court system and legal personnel to ensure that the legal aspects of family reunification are facilitated.

21. The agency works with the legislative system to develop statutory directives that support family reunification.

22. To ensure that highly qualified and well-trained staff members are hired and retained, the agency maintains collaborative relationships with schools of social work, advising them on curriculum development and participating in educational activities.

Practice

1. Reunification practice begins with an identification of the strengths and potentialities that exist within both the family and its external environment.

2. Reunification staff members view themselves as child and family advocates.

3. Parents are viewed as collaborators, involved in all decision making regarding their child.

4. Foster parents are active members of the reunification team; their roles and responsibilities are part of the case plan.

5. Foster parents are reimbursed for all costs incurred in relation to their reunification efforts.

6. Information-sharing and recordkeeping policies reflect family-centered practice and partnership.

7. Case plans are regularly reviewed and are revised in accordance with assessment results.

8. Case planning and case reviews use a team approach, involving all members of the reunification effort (i.e., family, foster parents, agencies, court, schools).

9. Children are placed with foster families that help maintain and reflect the child's racial and cultural identity.

10. Children are placed in close proximity to their families to better facilitate regular contact.

11. Children are helped to keep a placement diary to share with their parents during visits.

Directions*

1. Distribute *Handout III–1: A Definition of Family Reunification* and *Handout III–2: Underlying Principles and Guidelines for Family Reunification.*

2. Review and briefly discuss the expanded definition of family reunification and its underlying principles to help participants become acquainted with the proposed framework on family reunification.

3. Divide participants into small groups. Assign one or more principle statements on *Handout III–2* to each group. Ask each group to consider how the underlying principle might be expressed in agency policy, program, and practice in family reunification. Each group should record its responses on *Handout III–3: Building a Framework for a Family Reunification Program.* Before the small groups begin their discussion, review each of the eight principles for the entire group and give an example of a policy statement and practice strategy that would flow from each. Since the statements were written, in part, to help agencies develop reunification services, participants should be told that their responses will result in a partial set of the characteristics of a model family reunification program. For example:

    Principle #7: A commitment to early and consistent contact between the child and family is an essential ingredient in preparing for, and maintaining, a successful reunification.

    – *Policy*: In all cases where children are removed from their families, assessment of reunification readiness is conducted and case plans are developed within two weeks of placement, with particular emphasis on visiting.

    – *Program*: There is immediate, active, and ongoing agency support of visits between children and parents.

    – *Practice*: Children are placed in close proximity to their families to better facilitate regular contact.

4. Reconvene the large group and have each subgroup report on its policy statement and strategies. Record their responses on newsprint or a flip chart so that participants can see the emergence of a composite report representing state-of-the-art reunification efforts.

References

Fein, E., and Staff, I. "Goal Setting with Biological Families." In *Together Again: Family Reunification in Foster Care*, edited by B.A. Pine, R. Warsh, and A.N. Maluccio. Washington, DC: Child Welfare League of America, 1993, pp. 67–92.

Folaron, G. "Preparing Children for Reunification." In *Together Again: Family Reunification in Foster Care*, edited by B.A. Pine, R. Warsh, and A.N. Maluccio. Washington, DC: Child Welfare League of America, 1993, pp. 141–154.

Hess, P.M., and Proch, K. "Visiting: The Heart of Reunification." In *Together Again: Family Reunification in Foster Care*, edited by B.A. Pine, R. Warsh, and A.N. Maluccio. Washington, DC: Child Welfare League of America, 1993, pp. 119–139.

Maluccio, A.N.; Warsh, R.; and Pine, B.A. "Family Reunification: An Overview." In *Together Again: Family Reunification in Foster Care*, edited by B.A. Pine, R. Warsh, and A.N. Maluccio. Washington, DC: Child Welfare League of America, 1993, pp. 3–19.

Zamosky, J.; Sparks, J.; Sharman, J.; and Hatt, R. "Believing in Families." In *Together Again: Family Reunification in Foster Care*, edited by B.A. Pine, R. Warsh, and A.N. Maluccio. Washington, DC: Child Welfare League of America, 1993, pp. 155–175.

---

* If this exercise is to serve as a basis for program planning to enhance the agency's family reunification efforts, the instructor may want to develop a composite list from the small groups' discussions, and work with the whole group to categorize the policies and strategies into a scheme more useful for that purpose.

A DEFINITION OF FAMILY REUNIFICATION*

Family reunification is the planned process of reconnecting children in out-of-home care with their families by means of a variety of services and supports to the children, their families, and their foster parents or other service providers. It aims to help each child and family to achieve and maintain, at any given time, their optimal level of reconnection—from full reentry of the child into the family system to other forms of contact, such as visiting, that affirm the child's membership in the family.

---

* From A.N. Maluccio, R. Warsh, and B.A. Pine, "Family Reunification: An Overview," in *Together Again: Family Reunification in Foster Care*, edited by B.A. Pine, R. Warsh, and A.N. Maluccio (Washington, DC: Child Welfare League of America, 1993), p. 6.

UNDERLYING PRINCIPLES AND GUIDELINES
FOR FAMILY REUNIFICATION

1. Family reunification is an integral part of the philosophy of preserving families and of permanency planning, with their emphasis on ensuring continuity of care for children. Family reunification should be systematically considered and planned for by the child welfare and legal systems as early as possible in a child's placement in out-of-home care.

2. Family reunification is a dynamic process that must be based on the child's and family's changing qualities, needs, and potentialities. It should be viewed as a continuum, with levels or outcomes ranging from full reentry into the family system to partial reentry to less extensive contact. At any point during the child's placement in out-of-home care, the most appropriate or optimal level of reconnection should be identified and actively pursued. At the same time, it should be recognized that reconnection is not possible or desirable in some situations, and that those situations may appropriately require termination of parental rights. Even in such instances, however, children should at the least be helped to move into new permanent families with some tangible tie to their past in the form of pictures, a lifebook, or other family memorabilia.

3. As a form of preserving families, reunification embodies (a) conviction about the role of the biological family as the preferred child-rearing unit, if at all possible; (b) recognition of the potential of most families to care for their children, if properly assisted; (c) awareness of the impact of separation and loss on children and parents; and (d) involvement, as appropriate, of any and all members of the child's family, including members of the extended family who, while not legally related, are considered by the child and themselves to be "family."

4. Reunification practice is guided by an ecologically oriented, competence-centered perspective that emphasizes promoting family empowerment, engaging in advocacy and social action so as to achieve societal conditions and structures that enhance family functioning; reaching for—and building on—the strengths and potentialities of parents and other family members, involving parents as partners in the helping process; and providing needed services and supports.

5. Children in care, biological families, foster families and other caregivers, social workers, court-appointed special advocates (CASAs), attorneys, parent aides, and other service providers should constitute an ongoing partnership, promoted by effective teamwork. The differential roles of all parties should be clearly spelled out and understood.

6. Human diversity—for example, culture, race, ethnicity, ability—should be respected. Life-styles and child-rearing methods that might be considered different or unusual should be accepted so long as they promote a child's health and safety. This principle is especially crucial because a disproportionate number of children in care come from low-income families or families of color, whereas most practitioners are Caucasian and from the middle-class.

7. A commitment to early and consistent contact between the child and family is an essential ingredient in preparing for and maintaining a successful reunification. Child-family contact can serve as a laboratory in which both parties work on the problems that may have contributed to the need for placement and learn new ways to be together again.

8. Family reunification services should be offered for as long as they are needed to maintain the reconnection of a child with the family. For many families, intensive family reunification services may need to be followed by less intensive services. For a few families, some level of service may be necessary until the child is ready for independent living.

BUILDING A FRAMEWORK FOR A
FAMILY REUNIFICATION PROGRAM

Principle # __: _____

_____

_____

Policy: _____

_____

_____

_____

_____

Program: _____

_____

_____

_____

_____

Practice: _____

_____

_____

_____

_____

Module IV

VISITING—THE HEART OF FAMILY REUNIFICATION

- *Introduction to Visiting*
- *Visiting in the Initial Phase of Placement*
- *Visiting in the Middle Phase of Placement*
- *Visiting in the Transitioning Phase of Placement*
- *Making a Commitment to Positive Visiting*

UNIT ONE:

INTRODUCTION TO VISITING

Time	One hour
Purposes	This unit considers the range of contacts between child and family that constitute visiting and helps participants understand the purposes that visiting serves in meeting case goals to reconnect families. It also provides opportunities to bring out the challenges inherent in planning and arranging visits and to recognize the conditions—agency and personal—that promote positive visiting.
Suggested Audiences	Social workers, foster parents, parent aides, and child care workers
Handout Needed	Handout IV–1: The Purposes of Visiting

Key Teaching Points

1. Visits between children in placement and their families serve four major purposes:

   - reassurance (i.e., children know they have not been abandoned);

   - assessment (i.e., children's and parents' needs for help can be identified);

   - intervention (i.e., children and parents can learn and practice new skills); and

   - documentation (i.e., parents can be provided with feedback regarding their progress).

2. Visiting encompasses a wide range of contacts between children and parents. In addition to visits that might take place in a restaurant or an agency visiting room, visiting might include such activities as the child and parents going for haircuts together, shopping for clothing, or preparing a meal. Such activities foster a more relaxed time that will lend itself to building trust.

3. Planning for visits is often complicated and time consuming. The visit itself may be emotionally depleting. Visits, however, are the forum in which parents and children learn to be together again. Agencies need to promote positive visits through a range of supportive policies and practices, such as placing children in care settings near their parents, conducting visits when families can schedule them, and having children and parents participate in decisions about visiting plans.

Directions

1. Ask participants to brainstorm a list of activities that children and families can do during visits. Write their ideas on newsprint or a flip chart. Likely responses include:

• clothes shopping	• taking a walk	• haircut appointments
• food preparation	• class trips	• school conferences
• medical appointments	• household tasks	• practice discipline techniques

2. Ask the group to consider each of the activities listed in relation to the following questions:

  • How does the activity help parents and children learn to be together again?

  • If you were a caseworker or foster parent working with parents to plan each of these visit activities, what would you do to maximize opportunities for the parents to identify and respond to their child's needs?

3. Present the four major purposes of visiting as set forth on *Handout IV–1: The Purposes of Visiting*—reassurance, assessment, intervention, and documentation. Ask the group for specific ways in which visiting can accomplish each purpose. Note their responses on newsprint or a flip chart. Encourage them to offer examples from their practice to support their responses.

4. Distribute *Handout IV–1: The Purposes of Visiting*. Tell the group that even though visiting is the heart of reunification work, there are things about visiting that make it very difficult. Ask the group to name them and record them on newsprint or a flip chart. Likely responses include:

  • Arranging visits can be time consuming and complicated.

  • Last-minute changes can mean a lot of wasted time.

  • Observing family distress can be emotionally depleting.

  • Concerns about the impact of one's decision making on a child's safety can be overwhelming.

  • The threat of family violence can make workers feel personally vulnerable.

  • A lack of agency support for visiting can produce stress.

5. Ask participants to form dyads to consider ways of improving family visiting. Each dyad should produce six strategies, which will be shared with the group at the end of the exercise. The strategies should be broken down as follows:

  • two ways workers can demonstrate empathy for parents in planning and carrying out visits;

  • two ways foster parents or other caregivers can support positive visits; and

  • two policies that agencies should have in place to promote positive visits.

6. Record responses on newsprint or a flip chart to generate a composite listing of *Conditions that Promote Positive Visiting*. Likely responses include:

  • Place children near their parents.

  • Place siblings together.

  • Plan visits with parents' needs and resources in mind.

  • Foster parents can allow visits in their own homes.

  • Foster parents should look for and enhance parents' strengths.

  • Foster parents can help children work through their feelings following visits.

  • Require written visiting plans.

  • Keep caseloads low.

  • Provide flextime or compensatory time for staff responsible for visits so that visits can take place at times convenient for the families.

  • Have well-equipped, comfortable visiting rooms.

  • Provide financial assistance for visit-related expenses such as transportation or food.

  • Workers should believe in the capacity of parents to offer something positive to their child.

  • Allow children and parents to participate in decisions about visiting plans.

  • Train staff and foster parents on planning and carrying out visits.

Time	Three hours
Purpose	This unit introduces the three phases of foster care placement and the different purposes of visiting in each. Participants use a case example to plan family visiting in the initial phase of the child's placement, and to learn and practice ways to prepare foster parents and children for family visits.
Suggested Audience	Social workers, foster parents, parent aides, and child care workers
Handouts Needed	Handout IV–2: Case Example—The Parker-Vega Family
	Handout IV–3: Characteristics of the Three Phases of Visiting
	Handout IV–4: Considerations for Visits in the Initial Phase of Placement
	Handout IV–5: Practice Exercise—Visiting in the Initial Phase of Placement
	Handout IV–6: Preparing Foster Parents for Family Visits
	Handout IV–7: Preparing Children for Visiting
	Handout IV–8: Preparing Children for Reunification

Key Teaching Points

1. Each of the three phases of foster care placement involves different purposes. The main purpose of visits during the initial phase is to establish a relationship between the family, the foster parents, and the social worker. Visits during the middle phase involve family members and others working to meet case goals. In the transition phase, visits maximize opportunities for parent-child contact, and emphasize identifying and obtaining the services that the family will need to maintain the reunification.

2. Since visits in the initial phase are intended to build trust among the family, the foster parents, and the social worker, it is essential that the social worker, prior to and during visits, actively build on family strengths. This includes structuring visits to enable parents to demonstrate their competence, encouraging foster parents to look for and point out evidence of the family's strengths, and preparing all visit participants by informing them of the visit's purpose and what is expected of them.

3. In the initial phase of placement, children need to be helped to understand the reasons for placement, why they cannot go home with their parents following a visit, and what changes will need to take place for reunification to occur.

Directions

1. In advance of the session, distribute *Handout IV–2: Case Example—The Parker-Vega Family* (or have participants

use a case from their own practice). Have participants consider family strengths and what family needs are evident in the case.

2. Open the session by asking participants to share their assessment of the family's strengths and needs. Likely responses include:

   - The parents appear to have a genuine concern for, and attachment to, their son Alberto.

   - Alberto appears to have an attachment to each of his parents.

   - The parents have remained committed to each other for many years, through many ups and downs.

   - Both parents have a history of alcohol and cocaine abuse.

   - The family's support system is extremely limited.

   - The parent's financial difficulties prevent them from being able to afford adequate food, housing, clothing, and utilities.

   - The parents have a stormy relationship, with sporadic episodes of family violence.

   - Alberto has an attachment to his paternal grandmother, and she to him.

3. Distribute *Handout IV–3: Characteristics of the Three Phases of Visiting* and discuss the information in it. Note that this unit focuses on planning visits in the initial phase, during which activities are intended to:

   - maintain parent/child connections;

   - build a relationship among family members, the social worker, and the foster parents; and

   - engage in assessment and goal planning.

4. Distribute *Handout IV–4: Considerations for Visits in the Initial Phase of Placement*. Ask participants to apply the questions on the handout to the Parker-Vega case example. Alternatively, divide participants into two small groups, one focusing on "Relationships and Interactions" and one on "Assessment and Goal Planning." Each group should discuss visit planning and report out to the entire group.

5. Using the information on *Handout IV–5: Practice Exercise—Visiting in the Initial Phase of Placement*, have participants role-play the parts of "Mrs. Strauss and/or Mr. Strauss" and "Social Worker." The exercise is designed to help participants practice their skills in developing a partnership with the child's foster parents and in preparing the foster parents for the initial family visits. Depending on the experience level of participants (i.e., students, caseworkers), the instructor may wish to take on the social worker's role.

6. Discuss the exercise, emphasizing:

   - how participants felt in their roles;

   - areas of discomfort; and

   - how participants think the initial family visits will go.

   The discussion can be augmented by distributing *Handout IV–6: Preparing Foster Parents for Family Visits*.

7. Distribute *Handout IV–7: Preparing Children for Visiting* and *Handout IV–8: Preparing Children for Reunification*. Discuss the principles involved. Have participants apply the concepts by asking volunteers to role-play Alberto Vega and his social worker in various scenarios: having the worker explain to Alberto why he is in care, why he can not go home with his mother when she comes, and what will need to happen for him to return home.

8. Discuss the exercise, emphasizing:

   - how participants felt in their roles;

   - areas of discomfort; and

   - how participants think the initial family visits will go.

VISITING IN THE MIDDLE PHASE OF PLACEMENT

Time	Two hours
Purpose	Visiting in the middle phase of placement focuses on helping parents learn and practice skills to meet case goals, the involvement of other service providers, and the shifting of parental responsibility from the agency and foster family to the family.
	Using the Parker-Vega Family case example in *Handout IV–2*, participants will work with the family to develop a visiting plan and prepare for visits designed to achieve these purposes.
Suggested Audience	Social workers, foster parents, parent-aides, and child care workers
Handouts Needed	Handout IV–9: Considerations for Visits in the Middle Phase of Placement
	Handout IV–10: The Parker-Vega Family Goals
	Handout IV–11: Developmentally Related Visit Activities
	Handout IV–12: The Visiting Plan
	Handout IV–13: Practice Exercise—Visiting in the Middle Phase of Placement

Key Teaching Points

1. Visits in the middle phase are intended to help family members and others to identify the need for and involve other service providers, to work to meet case goals, to gradually shift responsibility for the child from the agency and foster family to the parents, and to assess and document progress.

2. Visit activities should be selected on the basis of the opportunity they provide to achieve case goals. For example, should a parent's goal be to better identify and respond to her child's needs, then the visit might encompass having her prepare dinner for the child and ready him for bed.

3. The social worker must be alert constantly to opportunities to point out the parents' importance to the child (i.e., he really misses you and has drawn a picture to give to you when you visit tomorrow).

4. Many parents are reluctant to visit because of the range of negative feelings that may accompany visiting, including guilt, jealousy, and shame. Social workers need to emphasize to parents the importance of visits to children, and underscore their own commitment to supporting parents through the difficult parts of visits.

5. When working with parents, workers should help them identify at least one thing they can accomplish during a visit.

Directions

1. In advance of the session, distribute *Handout IV–9: Considerations for Visits in the Middle Phase of Placement*. Have participants consider the questions on it in relation to planning visits in this phase.

55

2. Open the session by reviewing the status of the case and the progress made. The unit is based on the following assumptions about progress in the Parker-Vega Case:

   • The social worker and family members have established a positive working relationship. Ms. Parker especially has been willing to respond to the worker's efforts to plan goals. Mr. Vega is quieter, but participates to a workable degree.

   • Visits have taken place in the foster home; child and parents are asking for more frequent visits. Mrs. Strauss has been present during all of the visits, appearing friendly to, though wary of, Mr. Vega.

   • A case plan for the family has been developed.

3. Distribute *Handout IV–10: The Parker-Vega Family Goals.* Briefly review the purposes of visiting in this phase and the worker's roles (i.e., preparing parents and children, involving other service providers, assessing and documenting progress).

4. Divide participants into three small groups. Ask one group to devise a set of visiting activities to support goal number three, and to provide a rationale for each activity; the two remaining groups should do the same with goal number four and goal number six, respectively.

5. Distribute *Handout IV–11: Developmentally Related Visit Activities.* Reconvene the group to discuss participants' ideas, recording them on newsprint or a flip chart.

6. Distribute *Handout IV–12: The Visiting Plan.* Explain that it is a form that can be helpful to them in working with families. Using the suggestions on the handout for purposes and activities, and the considerations delineated in *Handout IV–9: Considerations for Visits in the Middle Phase of Placement,* develop with the group a plan for a Parker-Vega family visit.

7. Using the information on *Handout IV–13: Practice Exercise—Visiting in the Middle Phase of Placement,* have participants role-play the parts of "Social Worker" and "Karen Parker and/or Jose Vega." Following the role-play, have those who played the various roles discuss their reactions/feelings about their roles, the outcomes of the meeting, prospects for the visit, etc. The exercise is designed to help participants practice their skills in preparing Ms. Parker and/or Mr. Vega for a visit with Alberto as outlined in the plan developed above.

8. Provide opportunities to hear first-hand from the following participants in family visiting:

   • a parent whose child was/is in out-of-home care (The parent could be asked to share her/his feelings about visits, what helped or hindered positive visiting, etc.);

   • a foster parent about her/his experience with family visiting; or

   • a social worker who plans/supervises visiting (the social worker could be asked to describe how she/he helps to prepare parents and children for visits.

UNIT FOUR

VISITING IN THE TRANSITIONING PHASE OF PLACEMENT

Time	Ninety minutes
Purpose	Visiting in the transitioning phase of placement focuses on helping the family to develop a safety plan to protect the children from the need for future placement and building supports to maintain the reunification.
	Using the Parker-Vega Family case example in *Handout IV–2*, participants will work with the family to create a plan to protect Alberto from harm.
Suggested Audience	Social workers, foster parents, parent-aides, and child care workers
Handouts Needed	Handout IV–14: Considerations for Visits in the Transitioning Phase of Placement
	Handout IV–15: Approaches for Developing a Child's Safety Plan
	Handout IV–16: Practice Exercise—Visiting in the Transitioning Phase of Placement

Key Teaching Points

1. Visits in the transitioning phase help in the development and practice of a safety plan, provide maximum opportunity for parent-child contact, and build supports to maintain reunification.

2. The safety plan is intended to protect the child from future harm (i.e., the child is able to go to a neighbor's house if he perceives that his father has become drunk). Each family needs to develop and practice its plan prior to reunification.

3. In family reunification practice, the social worker should address only those problems that led to placement and avoid the tendency to focus on a wide range of family issues that, while important, should not extend the child's stay in care unnecessarily.

Directions

1. Open the session by reviewing the status of the case and the progress made. The unit is based on the following assumptions about progress in the Parker-Vega Case:

   • Both parents are enrolled in substance abuse treatment programs and a parent support group, and participate actively.

   • Both parents are employed.

   • Both parents are visiting Alberto regularly and are expecting to have him for one unsupervised overnight and one unsupervised day visit a week starting next week.

2. Distribute *Handout IV–14: Considerations for Visits in the Transitioning Phase of Placement*. Ask participants to review the questions as well as the purposes of visiting during this phase:

- to develop a safety plan; and

- to build supports to maintain the reunification.

3. Distribute *Handout IV–15: Approaches for Developing a Child's Safety Plan*. Review the material on the handout with participants.

4. Using the information on *Handout IV–16: Practice Exercise—Visiting in the Transitioning Phase of Placement*, have participants role-play the parts of "Alberto Vega," "Karen Parker," "Jose Vega," and "Social Worker." The setting is a meeting at which the social worker is to help Alberto and his parents think about what they will do if problems recur that could lead to placing Alberto.*

5. Discuss the role players' reactions/feelings about their roles, outcome of the meeting, and prospects for the success of the plan. Note that participants may show a tendency to want to address a range of family problems that emerge during the exercise. It is important to point out that it is the reunification practitioner's obligation to confine his or her work to those problems that led to placement (i.e., Jose Vega's intermittent presence in the home, while a problem for Karen Parker and Alberto, would not have led to Alberto's placement, and thus, should not prevent Alberto's return home).

---

* Option: The instructor may rotate who plays the social worker by tapping participants to take on the role.

MAKING A COMMITMENT TO POSITIVE VISITING

Time	One hour
Purpose	Participants have been exposed to many new ideas and techniques for using visiting as an assessment and intervention tool to help families reconnect and remain together. This unit will provide a forum in which participants can reflect on their learning, consider ways to apply the concepts, and make a commitment to incorporate new strategies into their practice.
Handout Needed	Handout IV–17: Making a Commitment

Directions

1. Open the session by explaining the purposes of the session and asking participants to form groups of three. Distribute *Handout IV–17: Making a Commitment.* Have them discuss their responses within the triads and complete the handout.

2. Reconvene the large group and have each person report out his or her responses. Note their responses on three sheets of newsprint posted on the wall. Responses to the first sentence should be written on a sheet titled "Obstacles," responses to the second sentence should go on a sheet titled "Practice Approaches," and responses to the third sentence should go on a sheet titled "I Can Make a Difference By…"

3. In line with the competency-based approach to training addressed earlier in this book, discuss the many benefits participants gained from the training, noting their understanding of the hurdles faced by family members on their way toward reconnection and their enhanced competency in using visiting as an assessment and intervention tool.

4. Conclude this module with a discussion of the ways in which participants now recognize visiting to be the heart of family reunification.

59

MODULE IV REFERENCES

Folaron, G. "Preparing Children for Reunification." In *Together Again: Family Reunification in Foster Care*, edited by B.A. Pine, R. Warsh, and A.N. Maluccio. Washington, DC: Child Welfare League of America, 1993, pp. 141–154.

Hess, P. "Case and Context: Determinants of Planned Visit Frequency in Foster Family Care." *Child Welfare* LXVII (July–August 1988): 311–326.

Hess, P., and Proch, K.O. *Family Visiting in Out-of-Home Care: A Guide to Practice*. Washington, DC: Child Welfare League of America, 1988.

Hess, P., and Proch, K. "Visiting: The Heart of Reunification." In *Together Again: Family Reunification in Foster Care*, edited by B.A. Pine, R. Warsh, and A.N. Maluccio. Washington, DC: Child Welfare League of America, 1993, pp. 119–139.

Illinois Department of Children and Family Services. "Visiting with Your Child." *Parents Guide Series*. Springfield, IL: Author, 1988.

THE PURPOSES OF VISITING*

Visiting provides reassurance to the child and family.

- Children know they have not been abandoned.

- Families know that the agency wants to help them reconnect with their child.

- Parents and child know that each other are well.

- Continuity of relationships is preserved.

- Psychological well-being is promoted.

Visiting allows for the assessment of reunification capacity and progress.

- Workers can assess parent's and child's willingness to reconnect, the strengths that can make reunion possible, and the family problems that can impede reunification.

- Workers can use visiting experiences to help parents identify family goals that need to be met in order for the reconnection to be maintained.

- Workers can alter the visiting plan to reflect family and child progress and needs.

- Workers can identify the need for informal and formal resources.

- The extent to which foster parents can serve as a resource to parents can be understood.

- Workers can identify children's and parent's needs for additional help.

Visiting provides an opportunity for intervention.

- Parents and children can learn and practice new skills.

- Parents and children can confront reality, recognizing what it really means to be reunited.

- Families can identify and test out their optimal degree of reconnection.

- Problems can surface and be addressed.

- Changes brought on by reconnection can be adjusted to the family's pace.

- The timing of the actual reunification can be carefully considered.

- Parents can be empowered by responding to their children's needs.

- Parents and children can express and work through their feelings toward each other.

- Workers can use real-life experiences to help children and parents.

Visiting allows for careful documentation.

- Recommendations and plans can be supported or changed through accurate recording of visiting experiences.

- Credibility of court testimony can be enhanced.

- Parents can be provided with feedback regarding their progress.

---

* Drawn from Peg McCartt Hess and Kathleen Ohman Proch, *Family Visiting in Out-of-Home Care: A Guide to Practice* (Washington, DC: Child Welfare League of America, 1988).

Handout IV–2

CASE EXAMPLE—
THE PARKER-VEGA FAMILY*

Participants

- Karen Parker, age 30. Caucasian, unemployed.
- Jose Vega, age 35. Hispanic, self-employed mechanic.
- Alberto Vega, age 5. In family foster care.

Reasons for Placement

Two years ago, the Department received an abuse referral from the Newville Police Department on behalf of Alberto Vega. Alberto had been admitted to Newville General Hospital with bruises that were at variance with the history given. Ms. Parker was arrested for risk of injury and drug-related charges. She was intoxicated at the time of her arrest. Ms. Parker denied the charges, blaming the injuries on the carelessness of a baby-sitter.

Alberto was placed in family foster care at that time. During Alberto's placement, Ms. Parker participated in a treatment program at Newville General Hospital, individual counseling at Catholic Family Services, NA and AA groups, and a Time-Out for Parents program at the YWCA. She also received the services of a visiting nurse and parent aide. After two years in the same family foster home, the Department returned Alberto to Ms. Parker's home.

The most recent referral to the Department occurred four months after Alberto's return home. A maintenance worker found Alberto alone and crying in a very hot apartment. He contacted the Newville Police, who then had Alberto taken by emergency medical technicians to Newville General Hospital for observation. Alberto was subsequently placed in family foster care.

Ms. Parker's explanation of the incident was that she had left Alberto with his father, Jose Vega, when she went

to buy a pack of cigarettes. Instead of returning home, she stopped at a bar where she became intoxicated and then fell asleep in her car for several hours. She had left at 1:00 A.M. and had not returned until 3:30 P.M. of that day. Mr. Vega explained that he had left the house to go to work, thinking that Ms. Parker was in the bedroom.

Family History

Father

Mr. Vega was born in Puerto Rico, where he completed the eighth grade. He states that he quit school because he did not want to take the mandatory English courses. Although he has had no formal training, Mr. Vega considers himself a mechanic and has had sporadic employment in this occupation.

Mr. Vega has had a 16-year relationship with Ms. Parker; they have never married. According to Mr. Vega, besides Alberto, he has eight other children from relationships with other women.

Mr. Vega's relationship with Ms. Parker is characterized by its inconsistency and dysfunctional communication. For periods of time, Mr. Vega will live with Ms. Parker and assist her with finances. Then, usually after a dispute, Mr. Vega will leave Ms. Parker's home and live for periods of time either with relatives or friends. Mr. Vega admits that their arguments get out of control, mostly when they have both been drinking. He says that he also has used cocaine, but that he does not use it very much anymore. Currently, Mr. Vega is separated from Ms. Parker and living in his mother's and/or one of his sister's homes. His other family consists of two sisters and a brother, who live nearby, and two sisters who live in Puerto Rico. The nature of his relationship with his siblings is unclear.

Whether or not Mr. Vega is separated from Ms. Parker, he has maintained an ongoing relationship with his son Alberto. He has a great deal of pride in Alberto, carries pictures of him, and expresses a desire to see him

* The authors are grateful to Edith Fein and the Reunification Services staff of Casey Family Services, who provided material on which this case example was based.

frequently. Because of his unstable job situation, Mr. Vega contributes minimally to Alberto's support. At times, this means that Alberto is without adequate food and clothing. Last year, Alberto and Ms. Parker spent a month in a shelter and then lived with a friend until Mr. Vega provided them with money for a share of the rent.

During an initial supervised visit, Mr. Vega spoke with Alberto three or four times and at one point sat with him on the couch and put his arm around him. Alberto recognizes Mr. Vega as his father and appears to have an attachment to him.

Mother

Karen Parker is the third of four children born to Donald and Lois Parker. Ms. Parker's parents separated when she was an infant and divorced when she was two years old.

Ms. Parker describes her childhood as chaotic and unhappy. She describes her mother as an alcoholic who was often emotionally and physically abusive toward her and her siblings. According to records from the Department, Ms. Parker alleged she was sexually abused as a child by one of her mother's boyfriends. When she told her mother of the abuse, her mother made the man leave the house. Consequently, the man hanged himself and Ms. Parker felt that her mother blamed her for this incident.

Ms. Parker lived with her mother until the age of 11. She then went to live with her father and her brother Donald. She lived there for two years but, because of disagreements, moved back to her mother's home.

By the time Ms. Parker moved back with her mother, she had already begun abusing substances. It was at this time that Ms. Parker's mother admitted her to the state hospital. Ms. Parker left the state hospital against medical advice and moved to Florida with some friends.

At age 14, Ms. Parker met Jose Vega. At the time, she was working illegally at a bar. She had no substantial means of supporting herself and Mr. Vega took her in to live with him. Since that time, Ms. Parker and Mr. Vega have had an on-again-off-again relationship. Ms. Parker appears to be more committed than Mr. Vega to their relationship. Even when they are living apart, however, Mr. Vega is usually available to assist Ms. Parker when there is an emergency.

As a result of her abusive childhood and early substance abuse, Ms. Parker never completed school beyond the eighth grade. Her employment has consisted of various unskilled jobs. She has worked at a dry cleaners, as a housekeeper at a motor lodge, and at a convenience store.

Ms. Parker's parents live nearby. At this point, she is estranged from both of them. There is a strong attachment between Ms. Parker and Alberto, who clearly recognizes her as his mother and looks forward to her visits. Ms. Parker feels guilty about her relapse into abuse of both alcohol and cocaine and has had difficulty in being truthful with Alberto about the reasons for his placement. Ms. Parker is anxious to have Alberto return, though she admits having difficulty with her parenting skills.

Child

In his brief life span, Alberto has had his share of traumatic experiences. As explained previously, Alberto was hospitalized when he was three for extensive injuries that resulted when his mother was intoxicated. During an examination at that time, extensive bruises believed to be four to seven days old were found on his lower back and upper buttocks. At that point, he was placed in family foster care, where he remained approximately two years before returning to his mother's home. Alberto's next traumatic experience occurred four months after his return home, when he was left home alone and unattended, reportedly for several hours. He was brought to the hospital and subsequently placed in family foster care.

Alberto appears to be relatively on target developmentally. He communicates well, although his speech is perhaps behind that of an average five year old. His pronunciation of words is not as clear as it could be.

When Alberto first entered the foster home, he had a few adjustment problems. For the first few days, Alberto would take another child's bottle, sit in the corner, and drink it. He also had some trouble sleeping the first few nights. Alberto progressed from this behavior to being attentive to other children.

The worker's observation of Alberto is that he is a relatively friendly child. He becomes especially animated when talking about visiting with his mother. He seems to be passive when it comes to expressing his needs or seeking attention.

Significant Others

Mr. Vega and Ms. Parker both bring Alberto to visit his paternal grandmother, Ms. Lopez, on a regular basis when he is home. Alberto has asked about her recently. Ms. Lopez is not aware that Alberto is again in foster care. Mr. Vega and Ms. Parker recognize that it will be necessary to tell her what happened. Alberto also has a godmother who is a friend of Ms. Parker's.

Foster Family

Mr. and Mrs. Strauss are Caucasian and in their late twenties. They have been foster parents for just under two years. They have a 12-month-old biological child. They are both active in their church, where they became interested in becoming foster parents after meeting other church members who have foster children. They see foster parenting as related to their religious commitment and look for other ways to express their care for those in need. So far, they have found their fostering experiences to be rewarding.

They have expressed to the social worker that Mr. Vega seems to be particularly untrustworthy and selfish, but recognize Alberto's attachment to him. They have stated that they wish to be helpful to Alberto in whatever way they can.

CHARACTERISTICS OF THE THREE PHASES OF VISITING*

The three phases of visiting correspond to the three phases of placement: initial phase, middle phase, and transitioning phase. Each phase emphasizes a different purpose. The most important purpose of visiting, however, regardless of the phase, is to preserve family bonds.

Initial Phase

- The family, foster parents, and social worker build a relationship.
- Assessment and goal planning are the focus.
- The phase usually lasts about 30 days.
- Family members are often uncomfortable with each other.
- Children are sometimes pressured (internally or by parents) to recant their allegations of maltreatment.
- Visits typically need to be closely supervised and controlled for location and length.

Middle Phase

- Family members and others work to meet case goals (i.e., taking parenting classes, going for counseling, etc.).
- Visit activities are chosen to provide ways to learn and practice new patterns of behavior.
- The agency collaborates with other service providers to deliver needed resources.
- The feasibility, level, and timing of reconnection is further assessed.
- Consideration is given to whether changes in arrangements or supports could be made to promote goal attainment.
- Visits typically occur more often, for longer periods, with gradually diminishing supervision.
- Visits may include a range of people who are significant to the family.
- Responsibility for the child shifts from the agency to the parents.
- The phase usually extends over several months, and can take years.

Transitioning Phase

- This phase occurs after the case goal has been practiced safely (i.e., overnight visits for a period of time).
- Emphasis is placed on identifying and securing the services that the family will need to maintain the reunification.
- Visits provide maximum opportunity for parent-child contact.
- Remaining stress points are evaluated.

---

* Drawn from Peg McCartt Hess and Kathleen Ohman Proch, *Family Visiting in Out-of-Home Care: A Guide to Practice* (Washington, DC: Child Welfare League of America, 1988).

 *Handout IV–4*

CONSIDERATIONS FOR VISITS IN THE
INITIAL PHASE OF PLACEMENT*

Relationships and Interactions

- How can visits be structured to promote the child's and family's trust in the social worker and foster parents? to maximize parent-child interactions?

- How frequently does the child need to have parental contact to sustain the relationship?

- Whom does the child define as family?

- What relationships are important to maintain or build through visits?

- What arrangements will minimize stress and conflict among family members during visits?

- Has there been any past history of parents threatening or harming the child, staff members, or others during a visit?

- How can visits be structured to:

  – help the child, family, and foster parents to form a partnership?

  – help the family understand what has happened and prepare for the future?

  – reflect the family's culture and ethnicity?

Assessment and Goal Planning

- How can visits be structured to:

  – assess parents' ability to provide for the child's safety?

  – demonstrate the strengths, resources, and potentialities of the parents and child that can make reunion possible?

  – bring to the surface family problems that may impede reunification?

  – facilitate goal planning?

  – involve parents and children in assessment and goal planning?

---

* Drawn from Peg McCartt Hess and Kathleen Ohman Proch, *Family Visiting in Out-of-Home Care: A Guide to Practice* (Washington, DC: Child Welfare League of America, 1988).

72

 *Handout IV–5*

PRACTICE EXERCISE—
VISITS IN THE INITIAL PHASE OF PLACEMENT

Mrs. Strauss and/or Mr. Strauss

This is your first experience as a foster parent and you have no idea what to expect when Karen Parker and Jose Vega come for their first visit. The worker has told you that the parents are very anxious to see Alberto, and you know that he has been asking frequently when he will see them.

You are concerned that the visit will be awkward for everyone. What will you say? What should you do? Will you stay in the room? What if the child cries? What if Karen Parker has been drinking, since you understand she has a problem?

The Social Worker

You are meeting with Mr. and Mrs. Strauss to plan the first family visit in their home. You know they are willing to host the visits but that they do have some concerns. During the meeting, help to bring out these concerns so that they can be discussed. Also, be clear about what the Strauss' roles will be during and after the visit.

Some key points to keep in mind when preparing foster parents for visits are:

- Encourage the foster parents to look for, point out, and build on family strengths, i.e., the foster parents might make statements such as: "With all the trouble you've had, I can see that you have always wanted what is best for your children."

- Help the foster parents appreciate and communicate to the parents evidence of their child's attachment to them, i.e., "He spent all morning working on this picture for you."

- Inform the foster parents of the purpose of the visit and describe what will be expected of them.

- Discuss any problems you might anticipate and consider possible responses.

- Commend foster parents for their commitment to helping the child and family.

73

 *Handout IV–6*

PREPARING FOSTER PARENTS FOR FAMILY VISITS*

Foster parents are important partners with the social worker and the family in visiting. It is the worker's role to convey this to them and to help them prepare for and be involved in visiting.

First, it is important for the worker to determine the following:

1. Are the foster parents able and willing to:
   - value the child/parent relationship?
   - allow visits in their home?
   - supervise visits in their home?
   - document what occurs during a visit, as requested?
   - provide transportation?
   - help to prepare the foster child for visits?
   - share with parents information and skills that are relevant to providing a safe home for the child?
   - maintain confidentiality?
   - recognize when they need assistance?
2. During what events in the child's day (i.e., coming home from school; after dinner) might visits be best planned?
3. Do the parents or the foster parents have prior commitments during which visits should not be scheduled?
4. Is the child saying anything about wishing to visit the family?
5. What visit arrangements are the parents requesting?
6. What aspects of the initial visits need to be recorded in order to develop and support case recommendations?

The worker should also help the foster parents to express their concerns about the visits, such as dealing with:

- awkwardness;
- a crying child who can't be comforted;
- a parent who is angry;
- a parent who has been drinking/is high on drugs; and
- sadness when the visit is over.

Finally, the planning meeting should make clear who will do what in carrying out the visit.

---

* Drawn from Peg McCartt Hess and Kathleen Ohman Proch, *Family Visiting in Out-of-Home Care: A Guide to Practice* (Washington, DC: Child Welfare League of America, 1988).

PREPARING CHILDREN FOR VISITING*

1. Children get preoccupied with details and self-interest. Be sure to inform them about everyday, ordinary details: "Where and when will lunch be eaten?" "Who will be there?" "Will there be toys with which to play or other things to do?"

2. Use references to time that are meaningful to the child: "You will be there on the day you don't go to school." "You will be back in time to watch Sesame Street."

3. Address any concerns the child may have about personal safety: "I will be with you, or just in the next room, during the whole visit." "You can leave anytime you wish; here is the number to call."

4. Help children to identify how they might feel once they are together with family members: "Some kids are nervous when they meet with their parents, other kids are excited, some are sad. How about you?"

5. Elicit the child's fantasy of what visiting with the family will be like. Correct any misinformation and respond to feelings: "Only Mom will come this time; Dad will be coming next time."

6. Use play, drawings, puppet shows, and other forms of communicating with children.

7. Children can be helped by being given permission to demonstrate to family members the ways in which they have changed and grown during placement. This can ease a sense of divided loyalty between parents and foster parents: "Let's be sure to talk with Mom about how well you can read now."

---

*   Drawn from G. Folaron, "Preparing Children for Reunification," in *Together Again: Family Reunification in Foster Care*, edited by B.A. Pine, R. Warsh, and A.N. Maluccio (Washington, DC: Child Welfare League of America, 1993), pp.141–154.

PREPARING CHILDREN FOR REUNIFICATION*

1. The social worker needs to address the child's knowledge gaps created by placement away from his/her family.

2. When explaining the reasons for placement and the expectations for behavioral changes, the social worker must demonstrate respect for a child's family, heritage, and history.

3. The social worker needs to respect a child's defenses when seeking information about abuse/neglect and when preparing the child for reentry into the family.

4. The social worker should be prepared with personal information about the child's past to help the child understand what has happened, sort out misinformation, and prepare for the future.

5. Attention should be given to enhancing verbal skills to aid the child in effectively communicating feelings, problems, and needs after return.

6. Attention should be given to maintaining varied and frequent sibling contact; such contact is a necessary ingredient for preserving the child's essential connections to his/her own history and family and will ease the transition back into the home.

7. In assisting the family in fusing individual experiences into a single family history, the social worker should create a forum for addressing and acknowledging individual experiences, changes, and expectations brought about by placement.

8. Before a child is returned to the family, the social worker must assist the child in understanding the safety plan and ensure an opportunity for practicing the plan.

9. In assessing the safety of the home environment and the appropriateness of reunifying the child and family, close attention needs to be given to the child's desires and concerns regarding reunification.

---

* Drawn from G. Folaron, "Preparing Children for Reunification," in *Together Again: Family Reunification in Foster Care*, edited by B.A. Pine, R. Warsh, and A.N. Maluccio (Washington, DC: Child Welfare League of America, 1993), pp. 141–154.

 *Handout IV–9*

CONSIDERATIONS FOR VISITS IN THE

MIDDLE PHASE OF PLACEMENT*

Social workers should consider the questions below when planning visits in the middle phase.

Relationships and Interactions

- How can visits provide ways for parents to attend to the child's developmental tasks?

- How can visit activities provide ways for parents to promote the child's progress on therapeutic tasks (i.e., the child challenging the mother's denial of abuse)?

- How can visits facilitate the parents' involvement in the child's daily care and special events?

Requests

- Have there been changes in the child and/or parents' requests? If so, how should the requests be understood and responded to?

Assessment

- How can visits be structured to:

  - provide a forum for parents to demonstrate increasing competence as caregivers?

  - facilitate progress toward case goals?

  - show the degree to which the problem(s) that led to placement is being addressed?

  - engage family members in an assessment of their progress toward service goals?

  - provide information about timing of the reconnection?

- In what ways should visit activities change (duration, location, activities, and so forth) to reflect the family's progress or needs?

- What do the child's and parents' reactions to visits thus far indicate about the family's potential for reunification? What do the reactions indicate about the worker's or foster parents' roles in the visiting?

---

* Drawn from Peg McCartt Hess and Kathleen Ohman Proch, *Family Visiting in Out-of-Home Care: A Guide to Practice* (Washington, DC: Child Welfare League of America, 1988).

Intervention

- How can visits be structured to:

  - provide opportunities to learn and practice new behaviors?

  - involve, as appropriate, other service providers?

  - gradually shift parenting responsibility from the agency and foster family to parents?

  - allow family members to express and find ways to cope with the feelings they may experience in preparing for reunification?

  - practice ways of handling a recurrence of problems following reunification?

Documentation

- What aspects of the visits need to be recorded in order to develop and support case recommendations? How can family members and foster parents be involved in documenting family progress?

THE PARKER-VEGA FAMILY GOALS*

Goal #1

Ms. Parker and Mr. Vega will not abuse drugs or alcohol.

Strengths and Resources: Mr. Vega has enrolled himself into a drug program. Ms. Parker has already completed phase one of day treatment and has been regularly attending AA meetings.

Goal #2

Ms. Parker and Mr. Vega will have enough money to pay for the basic needs of life, including housing, clothing, food, and utilities, and will manage their money carefully.

Strengths and Resources: Ms. Parker currently has a stable job. Mr. Vega is actively looking for a job.

Goal #3

Ms. Parker and Mr. Vega will set limits and teach Alberto right from wrong.

Strengths and Resources: Ms. Parker and Mr. Vega are motivated to learn new parenting techniques.

Goal #4

Ms. Parker and Mr. Vega will have a good understanding of Alberto's needs.

Strengths and Resources: Ms. Parker and Mr. Vega are highly motivated to visit with Alberto. They provide their own transportation.

Goal #5

Ms. Parker and Mr. Vega will develop a good relationship, free from abuse.

Strengths and Resources: Mr. Vega and Ms. Parker are involved in counseling to improve their communication.

Goal #6

Alberto will have opportunities to experience ongoing nurturance and responsibilities appropriate for a five-year-old.

Strengths and Resources: Alberto demonstrates an excellent capacity for attachment and the ability to cope with change.

---

* Prepared by Edith Fein, Casey Family Services, based on case material supplied by that agency's Reunification Services staff.

DEVELOPMENTALLY RELATED VISIT ACTIVITIES

Age	Developmental Tasks	Developmentally Related Visit Activities
Infancy (0–2)	• Develop primary attachment	• Meet basic needs (feeding, cuddling, bathing, protecting)
	• Develop object permanence	• Play peek-a-boo games
	• Basic motor development (sit, reach, crawl, stand, walk)	• Help with standing, walking, etc., by holding hand; play "come to me" games
	• Word recognition	• Name objects, repeat name games, read to child
	• Begin exploration and mastery of the environment	• Encourage exploration; childproof home; take walks; play together with colorful noisy moving items
Toddler (2–4)	• Develop impulse control	• Make and consistently enforce appropriate rules
	• Language development	• Talk together; read simple stories; play word games
	• Imitation, fantasy play	• Play "let's pretend" games; encourage imitative play by doing things together such as "clean house," "go to store"
	• Large motor coordination (run, climb, dance)	• Play together at park; assist in learning to ride tricycle; dance together to music
	• Small motor coordination	• Draw and color together; string beads together
	• Develop basic sense of time	• Discuss visits and visit activities in terms of "after lunch," before supper," etc.
	• Identify and assert preferences, sense of self	• Allow choices in foods eaten, activities, clothes worn
Pre-school/ Early School (5–7)	• Gender identification	• Be open to discuss boy-girl physical differences.
		• Be open to discuss child's perception of gender roles; read books about heroines and heroes together
	• Continuing development of conscience	• Make and enforce rules; discuss consequences of behavior
	• Develop ability to solve problems	• Encourage choices; discuss problems together

continued...

---

* Drawn from Peg McCartt Hess and Kathleen Ohman Proch, *Family Visiting in Out-of-Home Care: A Guide to Practice* (Washington, DC: Child Welfare League of America, 1988) and from Gail Folaron, " Preparing Children for Family Reunification," in *Reconnections: Program, Practice, and Training in Family Reunification—Conference Proceedings*, edited by B.A. Pine, R. Krieger, and A.N. Maluccio (West Hartford, CT: Center for the Study of Child Welfare, University of Connecticut School of Social Work, 1990).

Pre-school/ Early School (5–7) *(continued)*	• Learn cause-effect relationships • Task completion and order	• Point out cause-effect and logical consequences of actions • Plan activities with beginning, middle, end (i.e., prepare to bake, make cake, clean up) • Play simple games such as Candyland, Go Fish
School-age (8–12)	• School entry and adjustment • Skill development (school, sports, special interests) • Peer group development and team play • Development of self awareness • Preparation for puberty	• Shop for school supplies and clothes together; provide birth certificate, medical record for school entry; go with child to visit school prior to first day; talk with child about school experiences; attend school activities and conferences with teacher • Help with homework; practice sports together; demonstrate support of child's special interests, such as help with collections; attend school conferences and activities; work on household, yard tasks together. • Involve peers in visits; attend team activities with child (child's team or observe team together) • Talk with child about own feelings and about child's feelings • Discuss physical changes expected; answer questions openly
Early Adolescence (13–16)	• Cope with physical changes • Develop abstract thinking • Development of relationship skills • Become more independent of parents • Changes in peer group associations	• Provide information re: physical changes; be positive about and help with personal appearance, such as teaching about shaving, make-up • Plan for and discuss future; discuss "what if?" • Be open to discussing relationships, problems with friends; set clear expectations • Help learn to drive; assist in finding part-time job and handling money; support school completion • Transport to peer activities; include peers in visits
Late Adolescence (17–22)	• Separation from family • Develop life goals, rework identity • Develop intimate relationships	• Encourage independence through helping find apartment, apply for jobs, think through choices; tolerate mixed feelings about separation • Be open to discuss options, "think things through" together; share own experiences as young adult, both successes and mistakes • Be open to discuss feelings, problems, and plans

 *Handout IV–12*

Approximate dates effective: _____ to _____

1. Child's name _____

2. Visits with whom? _____
_____

3. Others who have visited; relationship to child _____
_____
_____

4. Visit purposes:

   • to learn and practice skills to meet the following case goals

   1. _____
   2. _____
   3. _____
   4. _____
   5. _____
   6. _____

   • to involve the following service providers

   Name: _____

   Relationship to family: _____

   Role during visit: _____

continued...

* Drawn from Peg McCartt Hess and Kathleen Ohman Proch, *Family Visiting in Out-of-Home Care: A Guide to Practice* (Washington, DC: Child Welfare League of America, 1988).

5. Activities that will occur to support the case goals:

Goal #   Activity

_____   _____

                 _____

                 _____

_____   _____

                 _____

                 _____

_____   _____

                 _____

                 _____

6. Visit length required to carry out above goals: _____

7. Visit time (Circle one. If appropriate, specify time.):

a. Flexible (to be arranged by parents and foster parents)

b. From _____ A.M./P.M. to _____ A.M./P.M. on_____

If relevant, is this a good time of day to meet case goals? _____

8. Visit location (Circle one.):

a. Parents' home

b. Foster parents' home

c. Relative's home

d. Agency visiting room

e. Other (describe _____)

If relevant, is this a good location in which to meet case goals? _____

9. Transportation arrangements: _____

10. Visit supervision (Circle one. If appropriate, specify supervisor.):

a. Visits unsupervised

b. Visits supervised by _____

11. Required or prohibited behaviors: _____

12. The following changes in this plan may be made with agency authorization (specifically describe):

_____

_____

Social Worker

You are meeting with Karen Parker and Jose Vega to review the visit plan you have developed with them earlier. A major purpose of the visits at this point is to help the parents to learn and practice some new skills in relation to their child. Review these with the parents and begin to plan with them for the next visit with Alberto.

Key points to keep in mind when preparing parents for visits are:

1. Communicate anything you know about the child's expression of the parents' importance: "He really misses you and has made a little present to give you tomorrow."

2. Address any reluctance to visit as something that many parents experience: "He may have a tantrum when you get up to leave, but together we will try to help him calm down." Emphasize the importance of visiting and your commitment to supporting the parents through the difficult parts of visits.

3. Specify the purpose of each visit: "We will have dinner together, bathe the children, and put them to bed. Let's see if we can help Alberto go to bed without too much fussing."

4. Make sure you let parents know what each person's role is during visits: "Ms. Richards, the parent aide, will be here to help us figure out ways in which the two of you can share some of the discipline."

5. Help parents to consider in what ways their reactions to previous visits can be used to shape future times with their children: "I know it was uncomfortable for you when Alberto turned to Mrs. Strauss for help in cutting his food. Would you like to have dinner alone with Alberto next time?"

6. Work with parents to identify at least one thing that they can accomplish during a visit, and help them to derive satisfaction from it.

Karen Parker and/or Jose Vega

You and your partner have been visiting your child every week for about a month now. Things have been going well (except for how much Alberto cried when you had to leave last time), but you are anxious to spend more time alone with your child without the social worker and you want to do more "normal" things together. You are meeting with the social worker today to talk about this.

 *Handout IV–14*

CONSIDERATIONS FOR VISITS IN THE

TRANSITIONING PHASE*

Relationships and Interactions

- How can the visits be structured so that members can practice, for extended periods, family life following the reconnection?
- How can visits be used to:
  - help the family prepare for the social worker's departure?
  - help the family and foster parents to clarify their relationship following reunification?
- How can visits provide a chance to review accomplishments and supports that can help the family remain together?

Assessment

- How can visits be structured to:
  - prevent premature reunification?
  - bring to the surface any remaining stress points?
  - enable the family and social worker to know that the reunification can take place?

Intervention

- How can visits be used to create and practice a safety plan?
- How can visits be used to strengthen linkages with formal and informal social supports?

Documentation

- What aspects of the visits need to be recorded in order to develop and support case recommendations?

---

* Drawn from Peg McCartt Hess and Kathleen Ohman Proch, *Family Visiting in Out-of-Home Care: A Guide to Practice* (Washington, DC: Child Welfare League of America, 1988).

 *Handout IV–15*

APPROACHES FOR DEVELOPING
A CHILD'S SAFETY PLAN*

Recognizing Hurt Cries

First time parents may be unaware of the different cries a child makes. By frequent visiting in the foster home with a patient foster parent, the parents can be taught to recognize the different cries and become aware of their child's needs. This awareness can be translated into more effective parenting when the infant returns home. Further, the awareness of a "hurt cry" can help a parent stop a behavior and try a different approach with a child.

What if

"What if" are situations that need solving. "What would you do if..."

Safety Probe

Encourage preschoolers to identify persons they could go to if they are being abused or neglected, places that are safe, and means of obtaining safety, i.e., use of telephone or going to a neighbor. Preschoolers should demonstrate an ability to carry out their plan through a simulation activity. It is not unusual for preschoolers and school-aged children to say that they will call a neighbor but have no idea how to dial a telephone or look up a phone number.

Saying Stop

When parents are emotionally overwhelmed, they are sometimes unaware of their words, actions, tone of voice, etc. If a child can say "stop" or "stop that hurts" the parent is sometimes "awakened" to their behavior and can leave the situation.

Signed Contracts

Teenagers can make reunification a challenging experience, even for the most dedicated parents. Teenagers should take an active and responsible role for a successful reentry. There needs to be an open discussion of the problems leading to placement, expectations for the reentry, and acceptable standards of behavior following reunification. A written contract can be a valuable tool in structuring the agreements and gaining commitments from all family members.

---

*	Drawn from Gail Folaron, "Preparing Children for Family Reunification," in *Reconnections: Program, Practice, and Training in Family Reunification—Conference Proceedings*, edited by B.A. Pine, R. Krieger, and A.N. Maluccio (West Hartford, CT: Center for the Study of Child Welfare, University of Connecticut School of Social Work, 1990).

PRACTICE EXERCISE—
VISITING IN THE TRANSITIONING PHASE OF PLACEMENT

The Social Worker

You have been working with the Parker-Vega family for 15 months, and have a good, trusting relationship with them. You want to convey to Karen Parker and Jose Vega your respect and admiration for all that they have accomplished in bringing the family together again. But you also want to help them prevent the need to have to place Alberto in the future. For instance, does Alberto knew the difference between beverages that are acceptable to drink (soda) and those that are not (beer)? What will he do if his mother begins to drink? How will Ms. Parker find the time to attend AA meetings? Can Mr. Vega assure her that he will take care of Alberto so that she can go? If not, who else might?

Karen Parker

You are really looking forward to having Alberto back home. You feel proud of the many strides you have made in being a good parent to Alberto. You have some lingering worries about your ability to abstain from drinking. You've done well so far, but you are taking it one day at a time.

Jose Vega

You are proud of the many strides you have made in becoming a better father to Alberto and a better mate to Karen. You wish that you could make a commitment to live with Karen permanently, but can't. Will things take a bad turn if you spend too much time together? Will Alberto be harmed if you need to go away sometimes? What does the social worker think? What does Karen think?

Alberto Vega

You can't wait to go back home. You think it will be fun—it's hard for you to think of going home as anything but fun.

MAKING A COMMITMENT

I think that one of the biggest obstacles for families on the path to reunification is ...

_____

_____

_____

_____

_____

Two particularly useful family visiting ideas or practice approaches that I learned from this training were ...

_____

_____

_____

_____

_____

One practice approach that I will try with families is ...

_____

_____

_____

_____

_____

Module V

LEARNING FROM A CASE STUDY

Purpose	The Cooper family case study provides a multidimensional perspective on the people, events, and issues that surfaced as one embattled family, separated by the placement of the children in family foster care, struggled to maintain its stability. This case study underscores many of the themes presented in this *Sourcebook*, which are brought out through a range of discussion questions and learning activities pertaining to permanency planning, family reunification principles, practice issues, and legislation and the media. References are included to enhance the participants' learning.
Suggested Audience	Social workers, administrators, foster parents, parent aides, attorneys, and judges
Handout Needed	Handout V–1: Why Are the Children Crying? A Case Study of the Cooper Family of Iowa

Key Teaching Points

This module is intended to integrate and provide further application of the material presented in Modules I through IV. The Key Teaching Points associated with each of those modules should be reviewed prior to the use of this module.

Directions

1. Provide ample time prior to the training session or class for participants to read *Handout V–1: Why Are the Children Crying? A Case Study of the Cooper Family of Iowa* and to consider the many issues it raises.

2. Select those discussion questions and learning activities that interest and time allow. The questions might be shared with the participants prior to meeting.

Discussion Questions

Permanency Planning and Family Reunification Principles and Philosophy

1. What major permanency planning issues and dilemmas does this case exemplify?

    Likely responses include:

    - family preservation vs. a child's right to freedom from harm;

    - parental rights vs. children's rights;

    - best interest of the child principle [see Goldstein et al. 1973];

    - psychological parent [see Goldstein et al. 1979];

    - a child's sense of time [see Wald 1975, 1976];

    - "reasonable efforts" [see National Council of Juvenile and Family Court Judges et al. (undated)]; and

    - placement with relatives (i.e., biological father) [For a comprehensive discussion of permanency planning, see Maluccio et al. 1986].

2. How did the following principles interact in this case:

   - the public's "right to know";

   - the foster parents' "freedom of speech";

   - the professionals' "rights and responsibilities to make informed autonomous decisions"; and

   - the right of privacy and confidentiality for both Karen Cooper and her children?

3. What are the ethical bases for the principles listed above? How would you rank order them? [For a discussion of the issues of confidentiality and privacy, see Lowenberg and Dolgoff (1992).]

Practice Issues

1. Reread the definition of family reunification and the eight principles underlying effective practice set forth in Module I. Discuss these in relation to the Cooper family as they might have guided the intervention from the child welfare agency's first contact with the family.

2. In January 1987, Judge Mott ruled to retain Karen Cooper's parental rights, and DHS began the process of moving the children 75 miles away from the Micks' (former foster parents) home to be close to where Ms. Cooper was being treated. In that the children had a strong bond with their foster parents, and a need for connection to their mother, what other options might have been posed besides that which Judge Mott selected? What agency policies and court directions would need to be in place to support the options proposed?

   Likely responses include:

   - Could Karen Cooper be moved to a treatment center closer to the Micks' home so that regular visits take place?

   - Could swift efforts be made to help Karen Cooper and the Micks develop a more understanding and workable relationship? Could similar efforts be made with Karen Cooper and her children?

   - Could Karen Cooper be given the option of regular contact with her children (who would remain with the Micks) versus being pressured into an either-or conflict (termination of parental rights vs. responsibility for full-time care of her children)?

3. In August of 1987, by her own admission, Karen Cooper's dream of reuniting with her children was fading, due to a relapse in her mental condition. Discuss the following:

   - How can practitioners maintain their commitment to the role of biological family as the preferred child-rearing unit in the face of serious and chronic mental illness in the parent?

   - How might the concept of "levels of reconnection" be used to guide work with the Cooper family?

   - In what ways did the stigma of mental illness influence support for Karen Cooper as a parent?

4. Discuss the rights of foster parents in relation to their opposition to a child welfare agency's decisions to move children in their care. What mechanisms should be in place to ensure due process?

   [For a discussion of one agency's procedure for a fair hearing, see Albert (1978) and Pine (1987).]

5. Consider aftercare.

   - What services might the Cooper children and their uncle and aunt need in order to remain together?

   - How, if at all, will their need for services change if Karen Cooper and/or Paula and Larry Mick maintain contact with the children?

Legislation and the Media

1. Is the mass media's interest and the legislative reactions to the Cooper case symptomatic of the public's frustration and need to "do something" in the face of child abuse and neglect? If so, how could the social service and court systems channel that frustration into more useful directions?

2. What role did the media, especially the *Des Moines Register*, play in this case? Were the implications of this role positive? negative? both?

3. What role did the media play in the formation of policy in this case? What are other examples of the central role the media play in making child welfare policy? What other factors influence the policy-making process? [For an extensive discussion of this topic see Hayes (1982), Nelson (1984), and Pine (1986).]

4. On March 31, 1987, the Iowa House of Representatives unanimously approved a bill that directed judges hearing child custody cases to "give primary consideration to the physical, mental, and emotional needs of the child." Discuss why this policy mandate is inadequate in the Cooper case specifically, and in reunification work in general.

5. Identify the laws or statutes in your state that pertain to family reunification (i.e., termination of parental rights, child custody, etc.). How consistent are they with an expanded definition of family reunification? Should they be modified to promote family reunification? If so, how?

Learning Activities

1. Twelve-year-old Anna, speaking for herself and her siblings, said, "We are going to do everything in our power not to go to Karen. If running away is what we have to do, that's what we will do…If we have to kill ourselves, that's what we will do."

Family reunification competencies needed to work effectively with the Cooper children toward reconnection include the ability to:

- explain the reasons for original placement;
- identify what has changed that might make reconnection possible; and
- describe what would be involved in working toward reconnection with the family.

Using a role-play involving each of the children and a reunification worker, explore what might happen if the above competencies were practiced. Be sure to explore with the children the idea of levels of reconnection, helping them to see that some form of contact with their mother might be desirable.

2. In December of 1986, the DHS social worker admitted that there were visible signs of abuse and neglect in the Cooper family in 1985, but added that the overt hostility of the children toward their mother began after they were placed with Larry and Paula Mick.

Family reunification competencies needed to work effectively with the foster parents include the ability to:

- convey to foster parents the social worker's and agency's commitment to working diligently toward family reconnection;
- facilitate collaboration and communication between foster parents and biological parents;
- accept and implement the concept of foster parents as professionals, as members of the service team, and as partners in service delivery;
- help foster parents to serve as resources to the biological family;
- help foster parents to identify and build on the biological family's strengths; and
- convey to the foster parents the importance of their giving the child "permission" to reconnect with the biological family.

  – Working in small groups, have participants write a job description for foster parents pertaining to family reunification and work with biological parents, including qualifications, essential attitudes, and a sample of duties.

  – Working in small groups, have participants design a recruitment brochure for prospective foster parents. Supply paper and colored felt-tip markers to encourage creativity. [Option: Tell participants that the cover should read "Help a Family Get Back Together."]

3. Slowly but perceptibly, a number of legislators, while becoming informed of the Cooper family case in 1987, began to see the value of family reunification as a desired treatment goal in out-of-home care.

   • Ask a small group of participants to serve as a public relations team of a national child advocacy organization. While the other participants observe, ask them to develop a set of strategies that the organization could have used at that time to maximize public attention and acceptance of the concept of family reunification.

4. It was learned in 1988 that all of the Cooper children had been placed with Karen Cooper's brother and his wife, who had long expressed a desire to adopt the children.

   • Ask the group to generate a list of possible reasons why this option was so long overlooked. After the list is generated, ask participants to come up with a set of practice principles and guidelines that would help overcome the obstacles they list.

   • Ask the group to consider other actions that might be implemented in the best interest of the children, now that they reside with their uncle and aunt. Might their mother have regular contact? Might Paula and Larry Mick have regular contact? Other ideas?

5. Develop a treatment plan with the goal of family reunification for the Cooper family as if you had assumed responsibility for the case in September 1986, prior to the events that became public later that fall.

   • What would be the major features of the plan?

   • What roles and responsibilities might the worker have? the parent? the foster parents? the children? other helpers? the child welfare agency? the court?

6. Develop a visiting plan as part of the above treatment plan. [Option: Refer participants to *Handout IV–12: The Visiting Plan*.]

   • What would be some of the key issues and challenges in carrying out the plan? How would you overcome them?

   • What are some of the activities that might be built into the visits so that they could serve the purposes of demonstrating and evaluating the parent progress?

   • Where would extended visits take place? What would a safety plan for the children look like?

7. In January 1987, Judge Mott ruled against terminating Karen Cooper's parental rights, and ordered the agency to reestablish regular visiting between Ms. Cooper and her children.

   • Organize a case conference involving the various parties in the case. Assign roles and instruct players to model positive collaboration in planning together.

References

Albert, M. "Preremoval Appeal Procedures in Foster Family Care: A Connecticut Example." *Child Welfare* LVII, 5 (May 1978): 285–297.

Goldstein, J.; Freud, A.; and Solnit, A.J. *Beyond the Best Interest of the Child*. New York: The Free Press, 1973.

Goldstein, J.; Freud, A.; and Solnit, A.J. *Before the Best Interests of the Child*. New York: The Free Press, 1979.

Hayes, C.D., ed. *Making Policies for Children: A Study of the Federal Process*. Washington, DC: National Academy Press, 1982.

Lowenberg, F.M., and Dolgoff, R. *Ethical Decisions for Social Work Practice*. Itasca, IL: F.E. Peacock, 1992.

Maluccio, A.N.; Fein, E.; and Olmstead, K.A. *Permanency Planning for Children: Concepts and Methods*. New York: Tavistock, 1986

National Council of Juvenile and Family Court Judges; Child Welfare League of America; Youth Law Center; and National Center for Youth Law. *Making Reasonable Efforts: Families Together*. New York: Edna McConnell Clark Foundation, undated.

Nelson, B.J. *Making an Issue of Child Abuse: Political Agenda Setting for Social Problems*. Chicago: The University of Chicago Press, 1984.

Pine, B.A. "Strategies for More Ethical Decision Making in Child Welfare Practice." *Child Welfare* LXIV, 4 (July–August 1987): 315–326.

Pine, B. A. "Child Welfare Reform and the Political Process." *Social Service Review* 60, 3 (September 1986): 339–359.

Wald, M.S. "State Intervention on Behalf of 'Neglected' Children: Standards for Removal of Children from Their Homes, Monitoring the Status of Children in Foster Care, and Termination of Parental Rights." *Stanford Law Review* 28, 4 (1986): 623–706.

Wald, M.S. "State Intervention on Behalf of 'Neglected' Children: A Search for Realistic Standards." Stanford Law Review 27, 4 (1985): 985–1040.

Why Are the Children Crying?
A Case Study of the Cooper Family of Iowa

by Vincent E. Faherty*

Perhaps no other child welfare case has received the media attention given to this one, beginning with a local news report from Kellogg, IA, on January 19, 1987. Until then, most Iowans were unaware of a foster care case that had simmered for more than a year and then erupted during the final months of 1986. The most memorable images of what would eventually be known as the "Cooper Case" bolted into the living rooms of many Iowans on that cold night in January. It was just a 40-second videotaped news report, but it left the two newscasters visibly shaken and barely able to resume their discussion of the rest of the day's events. What shocked the newscasters was the kind of scene that stays with one for many years, and even a lifetime: unsmiling state troopers helping social workers pull five children from the arms of a near hysterical foster mother, encircled by a group of neighbors. Except for the police and social workers, everyone was crying. A few were sobbing and gasping for breath.

The Cooper Case quickly evolved into a statewide issue that engulfed the public child welfare system, the legislature, the courts, the governor and several of his administrators, and the state's major newspaper, the *Des Moines Register*. Nearly every Iowa citizen was aware of

the case and had opinions about it. By 1988, the continuing drama within the Cooper family reached a national audience on the CBS television show "60 Minutes." Then, an even wider audience became involved in February 1992, when the family's plight was presented on the NBC documentary entitled "In the Best Interests of Children."

Information presented in this case study is drawn from public records, videotaped versions of specific events, and secondary sources, most notably editorials, letters to the editor, and news stories in the *Des Moines Register*, published in Des Moines, IA. It must be noted, however, that although an unusually large amount of factual material has been available for public scrutiny through the electronic and print media, all the facts in this case have not been, and should not be, revealed. Issues of confidentiality and rights to privacy are, and should be, paramount if the best interests of children and their families are to be served.

This case study, drawing from what is widely and publicly known about the Cooper case, attempts to present a set of complicated, and sometimes chaotic, events to illustrate the intricacies of family reunification. It focuses on the policy, legal, programmatic and practice aspects of permanency planning for children. The author claims no absolute objectivity since it was virtually impossible not to have empathized more closely with one of the parties during a particular event or, perhaps, with each one of the parties at some point as events unfolded. Thus, this work is dedicated to all those individuals personally involved in the Cooper case of Iowa. It is hoped that Karen Cooper and her children find the peace and stability they so rightfully deserve, and that the professionals involved learn from each others' accomplishments and mistakes so that the system will become better able to respond to the needs of more children and their families.

---

* Vincent E. Faherty, DSW, is Professor and Chairperson of the Department of Social Work, University of Southern Maine. At the time the first draft of the Cooper case was developed, he was the Social Work Department Head at the University of Northern Iowa. Dr. Faherty received his MSW degree from Fordham University in 1970 and completed his doctoral studies in social work at the University of Utah in 1976. In 1984, Dr. Faherty also completed an MBA degree at the International Management Institute at the University of Geneva, Switzerland. He was a Fulbright scholar in Italy, and has published in the areas of management, child welfare, and simulations. Dr. Faherty is currently producing computer-based, interactive case studies in conjunction with a federal grant on child welfare education.

Participants

- Karen Cooper. Mother of Anna (12), Amanda (10), Sara (7), Samantha (4), and Justin (2).

- Gerald Feuerhelm. Attorney for Karen Cooper.

- Paula and Larry Mick. Foster parents for the five Cooper children.

- Jane Harlan. Guardian ad litem for the five Cooper children.

- Thomas Mott. Juvenile court judge for Jasper County, IA.

- Gerald Sawin. County Director, Department of Human Services.

- Dennis Cooper. Father of Anna, Amanda, and Sara.

- Fred Walker. Father of Samantha.

- Charles Harvey. Father of Justin.

- Mike and Rhonda Butler. Brother and sister-in-law of Karen Cooper.

The case is presented chronologically starting in the fall of 1986 and continuing until February, 1992.

October 1986

Although it was only a short story tucked away on the bottom of the page, still, it was page one of the October 31 edition of the *Des Moines Register*, and the headline said it all: "Children Fight Plan To Unite with Mom." The story began with a description of a "typical problem family." The biological mother, Karen Cooper, was "mentally disturbed" and had placed her five children in the care of the Iowa Department of Social Services 18 months previously. The mother was now seeking reunification with her children. The Cooper children—Anna, 12; Amanda, 10; Sara, 7; Samantha, 4; and Justin, 2—were described as resisting the planned reunion "with tears and suicide threats." Jane Harlan, the court-appointed attorney for the children, and Paula Mick, the foster mother, were quoted extensively in the article. Both discussed Karen Cooper's mental illness, her deficiencies as a mother, and the children's negative reaction to leaving the Micks' foster home.

Karen Cooper's lawyer, Gerald Feuerhelm, refused to let his client talk to the press but assured the reporter that Karen was cooperating fully with the Department of Human Services (DHS) in order to regain custody of her children. The intermediate plan called for the placement of the Cooper children in two new foster homes in the Cedar Rapids area where they could be near their mother while she was in a residential treatment facility. The long-range plan provided for the permanent reunification of Karen Cooper with all of her children as soon as she was fully self-sufficient.

November 1986

In early November, a suicide pact involving the two oldest girls was uncovered. The girls had attempted to buy nonprescription sleeping pills at a local convenience store. When confronted by the suspicious clerk, the children blurted out their despair over their impending removal from their "mom and dad," Paula and Larry Mick. Gerald Sawin, the county DHS director, responded to the incident by expressing concern over the children's long-range welfare. Sawin further asserted that young children under DHS supervision cannot be allowed to dictate the course of their own future.

At this early stage in the case, no firm ideological battlelines were drawn. In fact, virtually all of those interviewed for statements—neighbors, school officials, and others—admitted that justice could not be served easily or quickly in the Cooper case. Discussions about the "best interests of the children" and "termination of parental rights" eventually appeared in the press, alongside those supporting the rights of a natural mother and comments about the proper role of foster parents.

While public attention to these issues increased, indicators of future conflicts began to surface. Within a period of approximately three weeks in November, a number of developments occurred in rapid succession, including the following:

- Jane Harlan, the children's guardian ad litem, attempted unsuccessfully to obtain an injunction preventing DHS from moving the children. She later successfully arranged for an early December termination hearing on Karen Cooper's parental rights.

- The *Des Moines Register* argued, in an editorial, for the termination of Karen's parental rights because of the "strong bond" between the children and the Micks, and because of Karen Cooper's alleged past abusive behavior toward the children.

- Apparently motivated by strong public pressure resulting from the *Des Moines Register* editorial and intense political pressure from Iowa Governor Terry Brandstad's office, DHS postponed the removal of the Cooper children from the Mick's foster home until after the termination hearing, which was scheduled for December 12.

- Citing departmental rules, DHS officials cautioned Paula Mick not to allow the Cooper children to talk with reporters. This raised for the first time the issue of confidentiality as it related to the Cooper children, to Karen Cooper, to the lawyers, to the foster parents, and to DHS personnel. Jane Harlan and Paula Mick reacted angrily to this restriction on the children's communication. Harlan stated in an interview on November 4: "If they (DHS) were proud of the way they handled this case, they wouldn't care who the children talked to." Paula Mick added: "I definitely believe the children should be able to say publicly, 'This is happening. Doesn't anybody care? Listen, world, I have a problem.'" Breaking his own self-imposed rule of silence, Gerald Feuerhelm added: "I still criticize whoever talks about this in public and tries to litigate this case simply by public pressure." Feuerhelm also referred to the "lynch mob" atmosphere he sensed developing in the community. Paula Mick countered by welcoming the outpouring of "public support" from the citizens of Iowa.

- The minister of a local parish in Kellogg, IA, publicly offered his church as a "sanctuary" for the Cooper children if they were forced to move out of the Micks' home.

- Two state politicians—one a Republican, one a Democrat—urged Iowa Governor Brandstat to intervene and re-evaluate the DHS actions in the case.

- Paula Mick announced that if Karen Cooper's parental rights were terminated, she and her husband would immediately file for adoption of the Cooper children.

- Karen Cooper's immediate family—her parents, brother, and two sisters—rallied to her support and announced publicly their belief in her continuing rehabilitation and ability to parent her children.

- In a scathing editorial on November 11, the *Des Moines Register* accused DHS officials of hiding their own incompetence behind the secrecy provisions of the juvenile court procedures.

- Citing laws protecting foster children and mental patients, Karen Cooper filed a civil damage suit on November 16, alleging that confidential information about herself and her children was made public. The suit asked for a total of ten million dollars in actual and punitive damages from Jane Harlan, Larry and Paula Mick, the Iowa Department of Human Services, and all involved print and electronic media news organizations. She also sought an injunction against further unauthorized release of information. On the continuing advice of her attorney, Karen Cooper steadfastly refused to talk with reporters.

- The Iowa American Civil Liberties Union (ACLU) entered an already crowded field of participants on November 21. The ACLU argued that the DHS "gag order" on the Micks and the Cooper children violated their constitutional right to free speech. Further complicating the issues, the Iowa Attorney General's office, representing DHS, countered that while state employees and state-licensed foster parents were bound by laws of strict confidentiality, foster children themselves were not.

December 1986

In early December the scene shifted to the juvenile court. The main players were the judge, various attorneys, and expert witnesses.

Jane Harlan and an attorney for the *Des Moines Register* argued for an open hearing on the petition to terminate Karen Cooper's parents rights; Gerald Feuerhelm and the attorney for DHS petitioned for a closed hearing. Assenting to the opinion that termination hearings should be closed only when both sides request it, Judge Thomas Mott ruled for an open hearing. In a second action, Judge Mott also dismissed motions filed by the children's attorney and Karen Cooper's attorney each attempting to disqualify the other. Harlan was claiming prejudicial contact with clients against Feuerhelm; Feuerhelm claimed conflict of interest against Harlan.

When the termination hearing began, the pathos intensified as the media captured and reported every graphic detail: Anna and Amanda pleaded with Judge Mott to break their mother's parental bond with them. Karen Cooper's psychiatrist testified that Karen's mental illness was controlled through medication. The DHS social worker admitted that while there were visible signs of abuse and neglect in the Cooper family in 1985, the overt hostility of the children toward their mother began only after they were placed with Larry and Paula Mick. Karen Cooper's mental health worker affirmed that Karen had regular contact with her children but noticed that she was also experiencing a steady loss of their affection as their placement continued. During her own emotional appeal to Judge Mott, Karen Cooper accused the Micks and Jane Harlan of deliberately alienating her children from her. Her attorney, Gerald Feuerhelm, charged that Karen had been betrayed by the very system she had thought would help her.

Staring coldly at Larry and Paula Mick, Karen Cooper is reported to have said, "If you had done your job, it would not have come to this." During this exchange, one witness later indicated that Amanda Cooper scribbled on a yellow pad, "I hate Karen Cooper." One news reporter present in the courtroom described the closing moments of this emotionally-charged hearing by quoting Gerald Feuerhelm and describing the scene:

> *"I feel bad about being involved in this. If the children want someone to apologize for what they've been through, I'm sorry. Karen's sorry, the human services people are sorry… I wish I could predict what will happen to the children," he said and sat down, rubbing his eyes and burying his head in his hands. Two seats to his left, Amanda Cooper wept, and Harlan comforted her. [Des Moines Register (December 14, 1986): 3B]*

In a move that seemed to gratify everyone involved in the case, Judge Mott postponed his ruling on the hearing until after Christmas so that the Cooper children could stay with the Micks through the holiday season.

January 1987

The headlines of the new year abruptly dispelled the holiday spirit of many Iowans. Judge Mott ruled not only to retain the parental rights of Karen Cooper but also declared that it was detrimental for the children to remain in the Micks' care. Reaction was swift and predictable: Jane Harlan appealed Mott's decision to the Iowa Supreme Court, and DHS immediately began the process of moving the children to two foster homes in Cedar Rapids, about 75 miles west of the Micks' home and near the facility in which Karen Cooper was being treated. Acting as spokesperson for her siblings, 12-year-old Anna said:

> *"We are going to do everything in our power not to go to Karen. If running away is what we have to do, that's what we will do. . .if we have to kill ourselves, that's what we will do." [Des Moines Register (January 6, 1987): 1M]*

In another lead editorial and with a sense of needing to do "something" in the face of this latest judicial development, the *Des Moines Register* issued a call to the 1987 Iowa Legislature to draft a "Cooper Law," which would guarantee that children's opinions must be considered in all future hearings to terminate parental rights. While politely received by several legislators, no visible support for such legislation was forthcoming.

The inevitable removal occurred in January. Paula Mick had agreed earlier to bring the children to the local DHS office, thus avoiding as much publicity as possible. For reasons that she did not share, Paula changed her mind and told authorities they should come to her home to get the children. As the social workers and police officers entered the Mick's small living room at about 9:30 A.M., they were met by a room full of photographers, reporters, and neighbors. Thus developed the wrenching scene that was starkly recorded and painfully broadcast that evening on local television news programs throughout the state.

The five Cooper children were led single file from the Micks' home into several waiting cars by a cadre of DHS social workers and Iowa State Police officers. Neighbors milled around uncomfortably and news photographers jockeyed for suitable camera angles and lighting positions. To say that the mood was solemn and that everyone present was either crying or trying in vain to hold back tears would be an understatement. The *Des Moines Register* reported the scene with atypical restraint: "With a flood of tears and promises to stay in touch by wishing on the 'brightest star in the sky' each night, the five Cooper children said good-bye Thursday" [*Des Moines Register* (January 9, 1987): 1A].

Thus began the public firestorm of attention and outrage about the Cooper case as Iowans sought to learn: "Why are the children crying?"

The *Des Moines Register* quickly condemned the removal of the Cooper children in an editorial entitled, "Social Justice Gone Sour…When society ignores the cries of its children, in favor of blind obedience to institutional regulations, it is far from attaining a true sense of charity or justice" [*Des Moines Register* (January 11, 1987): 1C]. In a follow-up editorial the next day, the newspaper first struggled with the core issue of confidentiality—"if caseworkers know something about the foster family or any other circumstances that mitigate against the children staying with the Micks, they are precluded from letting the public know by a state confidentiality law." Then, in recognition of the importance of confidentiality, the editorial noted that "wiping that law from the books is not something to be advocated lightly." The major thrust of the criticism was, however, the use of confidentiality as a cover-up for possible incompetence: "the trouble with confidentiality, however, is that it can mask stupidity and venality and prevent society from monitoring the institutions it finances" [*Des Moines Register* (January 12, 1987): 8A].

In a highly unusual move two days after this editorial, Judge Mott unsealed the proceedings of the December termination hearing and revealed his reasons for maintaining Karen Cooper's parental rights. Judge Mott publicly asserted that while the Micks did indeed provide the Cooper children with "security, confidence, and love...in the process they also served as poor foster parent role models and actively alienated the children from their biological mother." Judge Mott further wrote:

> *"They encouraged the children to feel alienation toward their mother and to hope that their placement with the Micks would be a permanent one. The children were vulnerable...Their foster parents violated their obligations and trust as foster parents. They did so in order to gratify their personal desires to have children."* [Des Moines Register *(January 14, 1987): 3M]*

In a public response to this, Jane Harlan blamed the children's alienation on Karen Cooper's abusive and neglectful behavior rather than on the Micks' caring attitude.

By the end of the first week of their separation from the Micks, news reporters learned that Anna and Amanda were living with a middle-aged couple while the three youngest Coopers—Sara, Samantha, and Justin—were placed with the couple's married daughter. The two families lived near each other, so the children saw each other on a daily basis. It was further reported that both sets of foster parents had several years of experience caring for foster children.

Back in the Micks' hometown of Kellogg, 35 of the Cooper children's school friends signed a petition and forwarded it to Governor Branstadt. The petition was a poignant appeal for the return of all the Coopers to their school and neighborhood.

On January 16, the *Des Moines Register* tried a new assault on Judge Mott's decision. The editor argued that alienation was a "natural" result when any child is placed with loving, caring, and concerned foster parents. There was almost an encouragement of such alienation as a treatment goal: "One wonders, given the circumstances, how the foster care they were called upon to provide could have done otherwise" [*Des Moines Register* (January 16,

1987): 14A]. The child welfare professionals in Iowa did not react to this editorial publicly, perhaps sensing that such a potentially explosive issue as "planned alienation" would best be left unchallenged and even undiscussed. Their strategy seemed to have worked, for this issue was never raised again.

The majority of letters to the editor and other comments from the general public were decidedly opposed to Judge Mott and DHS. Simply put, Iowans were outraged and saw the Cooper children and the Micks as victims of a brutal system. Gradually, however, a small counterforce began to emerge—many were foster parents themselves—who reminded the public that the absolute duty of foster parents is to encourage continuing contact between children and biological parents. One letter even described an ideal scenario in which Paula Mick and Karen Cooper should have worked together cooperatively, and the children could also have been actively involved in helping their mother be a better parent.

By mid-January there were growing concerns among some state legislators that the situation involving the Coopers demanded better legal representation. State Representative Dennis Black, a Democrat from Grinnell in whose district the Micks resided, publicly invited David Belin to join the Cooper case as a co-counsel with Jane Harlan. Belin was one of Iowa's most experienced and respected lawyers, and had served on the Warren Commission when it investigated John Kennedy's assassination. Jane Harlan publicly agreed with this suggestion, indicating that it was difficult for her to continue "battling" a group of lawyers representing the mother, the county, and the state. On January 20, Jane Harlan formally requested Judge Mott to appoint Belin co-counsel.

In an apparently related move, Representative Black introduced a bill in the Iowa legislature to encourage judges to consider the "emotional attitude...between foster parents and foster children when deciding custody cases." Most legislators reacted coolly to the proposed legislation, citing the legal principle that good law does not proceed from a single and highly emotional incident.

Something else was happening during this legislative debate: public officials were beginning to discuss, many for the first time, core issues in out-of-home care. Slowly but perceptibly, a number of legislators were beginning to accept the underlying principle of family reunification as the preferred treatment in most out-of-home care situations. As so often happens following public tragedies, other positive consequences developed. Broad and far-reaching issues within the entire field of child welfare began to surface in the print media, spurred on by advocates such as State Senator Charles Bruner of Ames, IA. Senator Bruner noted, in an article in the *Des Moines Register*, that concern over the Cooper children could bring about changes in the foster care system that would benefit the other nearly 3,000 Iowa children in out-of-home care. He also highlighted the numerous unknowns in the case, such as whether the child welfare agency had made reasonable efforts to prevent the children's placement in the first place; was the goal to return the children to their mother and, if so, what services and supports had been provided for reunification; and finally, how were the foster parents prepared for their roles as temporary caregivers and partners in the family reunification process [*Des Moines Register* (January 21, 1987): 3B]? Thus, against the backdrop of the Cooper children's plight, issues relating to early intervention, permanency planning, the selection and training of foster parents, and in-home services for abused children were introduced to an Iowa citizenry growing increasingly aware of critical child welfare needs.

During the last week in January, Jane Harlan filed a formal motion requesting that the Cooper children be returned to the Micks' home. In early February, Judge Mott denied her motion to return the children. Later that month, he rescinded her court-appointed status, thereby effectively removing her completely from the case.

March 1987

Anyone close to the situation assumed that interest in the Cooper case was destined to reach well beyond the borders of Iowa because of its sheer pathos, if not its broad implications for families. That national publicity occurred in early March when CBS television featured the Cooper family on "60 Minutes." Although no new facts were offered, the public was given a rare glimpse of Karen Cooper, who said at one point: "I'm their mother. I love them. I want a chance. I know I made a lot of mistakes." Under questioning by CBS reporter Diane Sawyer, the Cooper children seemed unimpressed by their mother's plea for another chance. They continuously referred to Paula and Larry Mick as "mom and dad" and related to their mother as "Karen." Perhaps the most direct statement was made by Larry Jackson, deputy director of the Iowa Department of Human Services. In describing the Department's opposition to the Micks' foster parenting, Jackson said, "Loving the children is one thing. Wanting them and coveting them is another." A CBS spokesperson reported that the network received an average number of phone calls about the show and that reactions were bal-

anced in support of both reunification and termination. Those closest to the case seemed to feel that the "60 Minutes" segment was both fair and balanced in its reporting of the situation.

Shortly after the show aired, phone and mail communication resumed between the Micks and the Cooper children. (DHS, without explanation, had ceased all such communication for a period of three weeks.) Based on this resumed contact, Paula Mick reported that the children were sad and depressed about their new foster homes. Meanwhile, other details about the new foster homes were made public. The Cooper children were living in two houses described as "spacious" in a "middle-class" neighborhood in Cedar Rapids. The two sets of foster parents were related as father/mother and daughter/son-in-law. Both father and son-in-law were ministers at a Cedar Rapids church. Contrary to reports from Paula Mick, the new foster parents described the children as happy.

On March 31, the Iowa House of Representatives unanimously approved a bill that directed judges hearing child custody cases to "give primary consideration to the physical, mental, and emotional needs of the child" [*Des Moines Register* (January 31, 1987): 1A]. The press coverage of this legislation implied that its origin was rooted in the Cooper Case, a view shared by the general public. Lawmakers took issue with this interpretation and steadfastly maintained that the bill was an attempt to make global improvements in child welfare processes, and was not directed at any judicial or administrative decisions made in the Cooper case.

A further indication of the dominance of the Cooper case in Iowa legislative matters occurred in the confirmation hearings for the new Commissioner of the Iowa Department of Human Services. Nancy Norman had been appointed by the governor just at the time Judge Mott made his decision not to terminate Karen Cooper's parental rights. In effect, Commissioner Norman inherited the controversy as well as Judge Mott's explicit reunification plan for the Cooper family. In early March her confirmation by the Senate was denied by a vote of 24 to 23; opponents cited her handling of the Cooper case and refusal to reveal information about it. The following month, with intensive lobbying by staff in the governor's office, she was finally confirmed by a vote of 35 to 15.

May 1987

On May 14, the Iowa Senate approved the child welfare bill passed earlier by the House of Representatives. One feature of the new, comprehensive legislation seemed to be explicitly related to the Cooper case: the court was mandated to consider a child's preference in any termination of parental rights situation. Even though most provisions of the law went well beyond specific issues in the Cooper case (such as allocation of more social work positions in DHS, mandatory six-month review of all foster care cases, an in-home services pilot project, increased foster care subsidies, and other reforms), the media continued to attribute the legislation to the case. "The law was born of the Cooper case's exposure of present shortcoming. It is good legislation. But the final decisions that have an incalculable impact on the lives and development of children fell to the judges and caseworkers, who must rely heavily on their own perceptions. We can only wish them wisdom in their lonely struggles" [*Des Moines Register* (May 21, 1987): 16A].

July 1987

Six months after being removed from their former foster parents, Anna and Amanda still referred to Paula and Larry Mick as "mom and dad" Both did admit, however, that their relationship with their biological mother had improved as a result of regular visits. The two younger girls, Sara and Samantha, referred to Karen Cooper as "mom." At this point, all of the Cooper children lived together in the same home, with the younger of the two related couples caring for them since January. The older couple had returned to a mission assignment for their church. Karen Cooper continued in treatment in an outpatient residential facility in the same city.

August 1987

Just as this family was beginning to exhibit some measure of relative stability, and just as the professionals involved were beginning to see some results from their complex planning processes, the family's fragile infrastructure collapsed again.

As a result of viewing a summer rerun of the original "60 Minutes" program, Fred Walker, a married accounting student in California and the father of Samantha, came forward. Walker publicly supported the Micks' home as the most appropriate environment for his daughter and the other Cooper children. Furthermore, he offered to seek custody of Samantha if Karen Cooper's parental rights were not immediately terminated. Meanwhile, during a court hearing on Karen Cooper's civil action case against the Micks and Jane Harlan, there was some initial concern expressed by her counselor that Karen Cooper

was no longer cooperating fully with her rehabilitation plan at the treatment center.

By her own admission, Karen's dream of reuniting with her children was fading. During the summer, she suffered a relapse of her mental condition and left the residential treatment center against professional advice. This development rekindled the Iowa public's interest in, and varied opinions about, the Cooper family. Professionals close to the situation decided that it was time to seek alternate arrangements for permanency for the children, and a wide and thorough search for either a long-term placement with relatives or an adoptive home began.

Concurrently, in a brief filed by Jane Harlan with the Iowa Supreme Court to overturn Judge Mott's decision to affirm Karen Cooper's parental rights, Harlan claimed that Karen Cooper abused and neglected her children even more seriously than had been previously reported. The brief contained graphic testimony from former social workers who chronicled instances of environmental filth, hunger, lack of clothing, and regular beatings in the Cooper home prior to the children's placement with the Micks. A second brief in support of these allegations was filed by a North Carolina-based group called "People Allied for Child Advocacy." This second suit urged the justices of the Iowa Supreme Court to terminate Karen Cooper's parental rights based on the retroactive force of the newly passed child welfare legislation.

A brief news item in mid-September reported that Jane Harlan was summoned before the disciplinary committee of the Iowa Bar Association and reprimanded for offering "extrajudicial" statements regarding details of the Cooper case.

October 1987

By early fall, the struggle to return the Cooper children to Paula and Larry Mick had taken to the streets—literally— in both Kellogg and Cedar Rapids, IA. Friends in Kellogg printed and distributed 2,000 car bumpers stickers containing five brightly colored butterflies and the slogan: "Free the Cooper Kids." The bumper stickers were widely distributed and displayed in Cedar Rapids, where the children were residing. Local newspapers reported that the children were prohibited from viewing the television news coverage of this development.

November 1987

Undoubtedly, the single most dramatic development in this tortuous case was captured in a banner headline on the front page of the November 27 *Des Moines Register*: "Cooper Kids To Get New Home." In a decision worthy of King Solomon, the Iowa Supreme Court, by a four to one majority, stripped Karen Cooper of her parental rights, and at the same time discouraged DHS from returning the children to the Micks' foster home. The minority opinion of the one (and only female) dissenting justice argued for a return of the children to Karen Cooper's care when she was able to provide for them fully.

In this publicly-released 21-page ruling, the Iowa Supreme Court recognized DHS' efforts to help Karen Cooper resume her parenting role but found her to have no realistic chance of becoming adequately equipped to do so during the remaining years of her offsprings' childhood [*Des Moines Register* (December 2, 1987): 9A]. The court also severely criticized Jane Harlan for her "inexcusable failure" to attempt contact with the natural father in this case, and for the "poor" quality of her legal services [Des *Moines Register* (November 27, 1987): 1A].

With Karen Cooper's parental rights terminated, attention shifted to the children's fathers as well as other relatives of hers, including her brother and his wife.

December 1987

By early December, attorneys for both sides announced that they would file independent appeals. Gerald Feuerhelm appealed to the Iowa Supreme Court to reverse its own decision based on their reconsideration of the evidence that Karen Cooper could become a competent parent with therapeutic support services. Jane Harlan appealed to the United States Supreme Court to overturn the Iowa Supreme Court's decision denying placement of the children with the Micks.

The torrent of letters to the editor of the *Des Moines Register* that followed the momentous court decision ran heavily in favor of Jane Harlan and the Micks. Typical of the reaction was this example from one outraged Iowan who advocated for a "common sense" approach:

> "*Give me just 10 minutes and I would put those children back with the Micks and pray they could love some of the hurt away. Give the mother visitation rights under supervision. The fathers could continue doing whatever it is they have been doing. Fire the social workers and the judge...they could draw their unemployment*" [Des Moines Register (December 5, 1987): 7A].

To many people, the next development on the case—though bizarre—seemed inevitable. In early December, it

was announced that the film rights to the story of the Cooper children had been sold to an NBC television production company in cooperation with Michael Rhodes, an Iowa-born television producer. Rhodes, a five-time Emmy Award winner, explained that the Cooper children would receive a substantial amount of money for the filming rights. The production was tentatively entitled "In the Best Interests of Children" and was scheduled to be released during the 1989 fall season.

Preliminary negotiations for the film rights were initiated by the children's lawyer, James Cleverly, during the spring of 1987. According to Cleverly, all of the major principals in the case—the children, Karen Cooper, Paula and Larry Mick, the DHS staff, several social workers and counselors—had been involved early in the decision to film the story. Cleverly further reported that many of the professionals involved believed that the television production would be "therapeutic" for the children. Eventually it was revealed that Paula Mick would receive royalties of $80,000 dollars; the children would receive $100,000 to be divided among them.

Epilogue

During the past several years, there has been little public information about the Cooper family. However, there have been a number of significant events involving the children and other key figures in the case. Following extensive court hearings, all of the natural fathers of the children were denied custody of any of the children, and their parental rights were terminated. The United States Supreme Court refused to review an appeal filed by Jane Harlan of the Iowa Supreme Court's 1987 decision. Karen Cooper's civil suit for ten million dollars in damages against Jane Harlan and the Micks was dismissed on the basis that malpractice suits can be filed against an attorney only by clients of that attorney. Both Jane Harlan and the natural father of three of the Cooper children individually attempted to become the court-appointed "conservator" for the children's finances. They were both unsuccessful, and the court appointed a new attorney to oversee a trust fund set up for the children's benefit.

Late in 1988, Nancy Norman resigned as the Commissioner of the Iowa Department of Human Services, citing undue criticism of the operations of her department in the Cooper case. Also in 1988, it was learned that all of the Cooper children had been placed with their uncle and aunt, Karen Cooper's brother and his wife, who had long expressed a desire to adopt them.

PART 4

SELECTED REFERENCES

- *Child Welfare (General)*
- *Child Welfare Competencies and Competency-Based Training*
- *Family Reunification in Out-of-Home Care*
- *Family Preservation and Family-Centered Practice; Preventing Placement in Out-of-Home Care*
- *Permanency Planning*
- *Race and Ethnicity*
- *Child Maltreatment*
- *Adoption*
- *Group Care/Residential Treatment*
- *Family Foster Care*
- *Adolescents and Independent Living*

Child Welfare (General)

Allen, M. "Creating a Federal Legislative Framework for Child Welfare Reform." *American Journal of Orthopsychiatry* 61, 4 (October 1991): 610–623.

Boswell, J. *The Kindness of Strangers*. New York: Pantheon Books, 1988.

Brown, J; Finch, W.A.; Northen, H.; Taylor, S.H.; and Weil, M. *Child, Family, Neighborhood—A Master Plan for Social Service Delivery*. New York: Child Welfare League of America, 1982.

Children's Defense Fund. *The State of America's Children 1991*. Washington, DC: Author, 1991.

Costin, L.B.; Bell, C.J.; and Downs, S.W. *Child Welfare: Policy and Practice* (4th ed.). New York: Longman, 1991.

Goldstein, J.; Freud, A.; and Solnit, A.J. *Beyond the Best Interests of the Child*. New York: The Free Press, 1973.

Goldstein, J.; Freud, A.; and Solnit, A.J. *Before the Best Interests of the Child*. New York: The Free Press, 1979.

Hayes, C.D., ed. *Making Policies for Children: A Study of the Federal Process*. Washington, DC: National Academy Press, 1982.

Hudson, J., and Galaway, B., eds. *The State as Parent—International Perspectives on Intervention with Young People*. Dordrecht, The Netherlands: Kluwer Academic Publishers, 1989.

Janchill, Sr. Mary Paul. *Guidelines to Decision-Making in Child Welfare*. New York: Human Services Workshops, 1981.

Kadushin, A., and Martin, J. *Child Welfare Services* (4th ed.). New York: Macmillan Publishing Co., 1988.

Kamerman, S.B., and Kahn, A.J. *Social Services for Children, Youth and Families in the United States*. New York: Pergamon Press, 1990.

Knitzer, J., and Allen, M. *Children without Homes: An Examination of Public Responsibility to Children in Out-of-Home Care*. Washington, DC: Children's Defense Fund, 1978.

Laird, J., and Hartman, A., eds. *A Handbook of Child Welfare:* *Context, Knowledge, and Practice*. New York: The Free Press, 1985.

Maidman, F., ed. *Child Welfare: A Source Book of Knowledge and Practice*. New York: Child Welfare League of America, 1984.

Maluccio, A.N. "The Optimism of Policy Choices in Child Welfare." *American Journal of Orthopsychiatry* 61, 4 (October 1991): 606–609.

Maluccio, A.N.; Fein, E.; and Olmstead, K.A. *Permanency Planning for Children: Concepts and Methods*. London and New York: Routledge, Chapman, and Hall, 1986.

McGowan, B.B., and Meezan, W., eds. *Child Welfare: Current Dilemmas—Future Directions*. Itasca, IL: F.E. Peacock Publishers, 1983.

Mech, E.V. "Out-of-Home Placement Rates." *Social Service Review* 57, 4 (December 1983): 659–667.

Miller, J. "Child Welfare Reform and the Role of Women." *American Journal of Orthopsychiatry* 61, 4 (October 1991): 592–598.

National Commission on Children. *Beyond Rhetoric: A New American Agenda for Children and Families*. Washington, DC: Author, 1991.

Pecora, P.; Whittaker, J.K.; and Maluccio, A.N. *The Child Welfare Challenge: Policy, Practice, and Research*. New York: Aldine de Gruyter, 1992.

Pelton, L.H. *For Reasons of Poverty: A Critical Analysis of the Public Child Welfare System in the United States*. New York: Praeger Publishers, 1989.

Pine, B.A. "Child Welfare Reform and the Political Process." *Social Service Review* 60, 3 (September 1986): 339–359.

Select Committee on Children, Youth and Families, U.S. House of Representatives. *No Place to Call Home: Discarded Children in America*. Washington, DC: U.S. Government Printing Office, 1989.

Stein, T.J., and Rzepnicki, T.L. *Decision Making at Child Welfare Intake*. New York: Child Welfare League of America, 1983.

Stein, T.J. *Child Welfare and the Law*. New York: Longman, 1991.

Whittaker, J.K.; Schinke, S.D.; and Gilchrist, L.D. "The Ecological Paradigm in Child, Youth, and Family Services: Implications for Policy and Practice." *Social Service Review* 60, 4 (December 1986): 483–503.

Child Welfare Competencies and Competency-Based Training

American Public Welfare Association. *A Guide to Delivery of Child Protective Services: Analysis of the Tasks, Knowledge and Skill Requisites and Performance Criteria of the Child Protective Functions.* Washington, DC: Author, 1981.

Brook, P.A. "Applying Adult Learning Principles to Competency Based Staff Development." *Canadian Vocational Journal* 24, 4 (April 1989): 4–6.

Dennis-Small, L. *Advanced Job Skills Training Project Annual Report: Innovations in Protective Services.* Austin, TX: Texas State Department of Human Resources, 1985.

Hughes, R.C., and Rycus, J.S. *Target: Competent Staff—Competency-Based Inservice Training for Child Welfare.* Washington, DC: Child Welfare League of America, and Columbus, OH: The Institute for Human Services, 1989.

Kaufman, R., and Sample, J. "Defining Functional Competencies for Training and Performance Development." *Educational Technology* 26, 3 (March 1986): 16–21.

Pine, B.A.; Warsh, R.; and Maluccio, A.N. "Training for Competence in Family Reunification Practice." In *Together Again: Family Reunification in Foster Care*, edited by B.A. Pine, R. Warsh, and A.N. Maluccio. Washington, DC: Child Welfare League of America, 1993, pp. 35–50.

School, S.S., and McQueen, P. "The Basic Skills Articulation Plan: Curriculum Development Through Staff Development." *Journal of Staff Development* 6, 2 (October 1985): 138–142.

Sims, R.R.; Veres, J.G.; and Heninger, S.M. "Training for Competence." *Public Personnel Management* 18, 1 (Spring 1989): 101–107.

University of Kentucky, College of Social Work. *Collaboration for Competency: Examining Social Work Curriculum in the Perspective of Current Practice with Children and Families.* Lexington, KY: Author, 1989.

Washington, R.O.; Rindfleisch, N.J.; Toomey, B.; Bushnell, J.; and Pecora, P. *A Report of the Ohio-Wisconsin Children's Services Training Needs Assessment Project.* Columbus, OH: College of Social Work, Ohio State University, undated.

Wood, R., and Power, C. "Aspects of the Competence-Performance Distinction: Educational, Psychological and Measurement Issues." *Journal of Curriculum Studies* 19, 5 (September–October 1987): 409–424.

Family Reunification in Out-of-Home Care

Abramczyk, L.W., and Ross, J.W., eds. *International Reunification Symposium.* Columbia, SC: University of South Carolina College of Social Work, 1993.

Aldgate, J.; Pratt, R.; and Duggan, M. "Using Care Away from Home to Prevent Family Breakdown." *Adoption and Fostering* 13, 2 (1989): 32–37.

Aldgate, J.; Maluccio, A.; and Reeves, C. *Adolescents in Foster Families.* London: B.T. Batsford, and Chicago: Lyceum Books, 1989.

Barth, R.P., and Berry, M. "Outcomes of Child Welfare Services under Permanency Planning." *Social Service Review* 61, 1 (March 1987): 71–90.

Block, N.M. "Toward Reducing Recidivism in Foster Care." *Child Welfare* LX, 9 (November 1981): 597–610.

Blumenthal, K., and Weinberg, A. "Issues Concerning Parental Visiting of Children in Foster Care." In *Foster Children in the Courts*, edited by M. Hardin. Boston: Butterworth Legal Publishers, 1983, pp. 372–398.

Blumenthal, K., and Weinberg, A., eds. *Establishing Parent Involvement in Foster Care Agencies.* New York: Child Welfare League of America, 1984.

Bryce, M., and Lloyd, J.C., eds. *Treating Families in the Home—An Alternative to Placement.* Springfield, IL: Charles C Thomas, 1981.

Carlo, P., and Shennum, W.A. "Family Reunification Efforts that Work: A Three Year Follow-up Study of Children in Residential Treatment." *Child and Adolescent Social Work* 6, 3 (Fall 1989): 211–216.

Carlo, P. "The Children's Residential Treatment Center as a Living Laboratory for Family Members: A Review of the Literature and Its Implications for Practice." *Child Care Quarterly* 14, 3 (Fall 1985): 156–170.

Carlo, P. "Implementing a Parent Involvement/Parent Education Program in a Children's Residential Treatment Center." *Child and Youth Care Quarterly* 17, 3 (Fall 1988): 195–206.

Carlo, P. "Parent Education vs. Parent Involvement: Which Type of Efforts Work Best to Reunify Families?" *Journal of Social Service Research* 17, 1/2 (1993): 135–150.

Child Welfare League of America. *Standards for Services to

Strengthen and Preserve Families with Children. Washington, DC: Author, 1990.

Cole, E., and Duva, J. *Family Preservation: An Orientation for Administrators and Practitioners.* Washington, DC: Child Welfare League of America, 1990.

Edna McConnell Clark Foundation. *Keeping Families Together: The Case for Family Preservation.* New York: Author, 1985.

Falk, R. "Family Reunification in a Residential Facility." *Residential Treatment for Children and Youth* 7, 3 (1990): 39–49.

Fein, E.; Maluccio, A.N.; Hamilton, V.J.; and Ward, D. "After Foster Care: Outcomes of Permanency Planning for Children." *Child Welfare* LXII, 6 (November–December 1983): 485–558.

Fein, E.; Maluccio, A.N.; and Kluger, M. *No More Partings— An Examination of Long-Term Foster Family Care.* Washington, DC: Child Welfare League of America, 1990.

Fein, E., and Staff, I. "Last Best Chance: Findings from a Reunification Services Program." *Child Welfare* LXXII, 1 (January–February 1993): 25–40.

Fein, E., and Staff, I. "Implementing Reunification Services." *Families in Society* 72, 6 (June 1991): 335–343.

Goerge R.M. "The Reunification Process in Substitute Care." *Social Service Review* 64, 3 (September 1990): 422–457.

Hardin, M., ed. *Foster Children in the Courts.* Boston, MA: Butterworth Legal Publishers, 1983.

Hess, P.M., and Proch, K.O. *Family Visiting in Out-of-Home Care: A Guide to Practice.* Washington, DC: Child Welfare League of America, 1988.

Horejsi, C.R.; Bertsche, A.V.; and Clark, F.W. *Social Work Practice with Parents of Children in Foster Care—A Handbook.* Springfield, IL: Charles C Thomas, 1981.

Jones, M.A. *A Second Chance for Families: Five Years Later.* New York: Child Welfare League of America, 1985.

Kadushin, A., and Martin, J.A. *Child Welfare Services* (4th ed.). New York: Macmillan Publishing Co, 1988.

Kagan, R., and Schlosberg, S. *Families in Perpetual Crisis.* New York: W.W. Norton, 1989.

Kaplan, L. *Working with Multi-Problem Families.* Lexington, MA: Lexington Books, 1986.

Kelsall, J., and McCullough, B. *Family Work in Residential Child Care: Partnership in Practice.* Cheadle, England: Boys' and Girls' Welfare Society, 1988.

Lloyd, J.C., and Bryce, M.E. *Placement Prevention and Family Reunification: A Handbook for the Family-Centered Practitioner* (rev.). Iowa City, IA: National Resource Center on Family Based Services, The University of Iowa School of Social Work, 1984.

Maluccio, A.N., and Sinanoglu, P.A., eds. *The Challenge of Partnership: Working with Parents of Children in Foster Care.* New York: Child Welfare League of America, 1981.

Maluccio, A.N.; Fein, E.; and Olmstead, K.A. *Permanency Planning for Children: Concepts and Methods.* London and New York: Routledge, Chapman, and Hall, 1986.

Maluccio, A.N.; Krieger, R.; and Pine, B.A. *Reconnecting Families: Family Reunification Competencies for Social Workers.* West Hartford, CT: Center for the Study of Child Welfare, The University of Connecticut School of Social Work, 1990.

Maluccio, A.N.; Krieger, R.; and Pine, B.A. "Preserving Families through Family Reunification." In *Intensive Family Preservation Services: An Instructional Sourcebook,* edited by E.M. Tracy, D.A. Haapala, J. Kinney, and P.J. Pecora. Cleveland, OH: Case Western Reserve University, Mandel School of Applied Social Services, 1991, pp. 215–235.

Maluccio, A.N., and Whittaker, J.K. "Helping the Biological Families of Children in Out-of-Home Placement." In *Troubled Relationships,* edited by E.W. Nunnally, C.S. Chilman, and F.M. Cox. Newbury Park, CA: Sage Publications, 1988, pp. 205–217.

Maybanks, S., and Bryce, M.E., eds. *Home-Based Services for Children and Families: Policy, Practice, and Research.* Springfield, IL: Charles C Thomas, 1979.

McGowan, B.G., and Meezan, W., eds. *Child Welfare: Current Dilemmas—Future Directions.* Itasca, IL: F.E. Peacock Publishers, 1983.

Millham, S.; Bullock, R.; Hosie, K.; and Haak, M. *Children Lost in Care: The Family Contact of Children in Care.* Farnborough, England: Gower, 1986.

Millham, S.; Bullock, R.; Hosie, K.; and Haak, M. *Lost in Care: The Problems of Maintaining Links between Children in Care and Their Families.* Aldershot, England: Gower, 1986.

Pike, V.; Downs, S. Emlen, A.; Downs, G.; and Case, D. *Permanent Planning for Children in Foster Care: A Handbook for Social Workers.* Washington, DC: U.S. Department of Health, Education, and Welfare, Publication No. (OHDS) 78–30124, 1977.

Pine, B.A.; Krieger, R.; and Maluccio, A.N., eds. *Reconnections: Program, Practice, and Training in Family Reunification—Conference Proceedings.* West Hartford, CT: Center for the Study of Child Welfare, The University of Connecticut School of Social Work, 1990.

Pine, B.A.; Warsh, R.; and Maluccio, A.N., eds. *Together Again: Family Reunification in Foster Care*, Washington, DC: Child Welfare League of America, 1993.

Ratterman, D. "Detrimental to the Best Interests of the Child: When the Agency's Failure to Make Diligent Efforts or Allow Visitation Can be Excused in a Termination Action." *Children's Legal Rights Journal* 11, 2 (Summer 1990): 2–7.

Rosenberg, L.A. "Psychological Factors in Separation and Reunification: The Needs of the Child and of the Family." *Children's Legal Rights Journal* 12, 1 (Winter 1991): 20–24.

Rzepnicki, T.L. "Recidivism of Foster Children Returned to Their Own Homes: A Review and New Directions for Research." *Social Service Review* 61, 1 (March 1987): 56–70.

Rowe, J.; Cain, H.; Hundleby, M.; and Keane, A. *Long-Term Foster Care*. London: Batsford/British Agencies for Adoption and Fostering, 1984.

Rowe, J.; Hundleby, M.; and Garnett, L. *Child Care Now—A Survey of Placement Patterns*. London: British Agencies for Adoption and Fostering, 1989.

Simms, M.D., and Bolden, B.J. "The Family Reunification Project: Facilitating Regular Contact Among Foster Children, Biological Families, and Foster Families." *Child Welfare* LXX, 6 (November–December 1991): 679–690.

Sinanoglu, P.A., and Maluccio, A.N., eds. *Parents of Children in Placement: Perspectives and Programs*. New York: Child Welfare League of America, 1981.

Stein, T.J.; Gambrill, E.D.; and Wiltse, K.T. *Children in Placement: Perspectives and Programs*. New York: Praeger Publishers, 1978.

Stein, T.J. *Child Welfare and the Law*. New York: Longman, 1991.

Thoburn, J. *Success and Failure in Permanent Family Placement*. Aldershot, England: Gower Publishing Co., 1990.

Triseliotis, J., ed. *New Developments in Foster Care and Adoption*. London: Routledge and Kegan, Paul, 1980.

Turner, J. "Reuniting Children in Care with their Biological Parents." *Social Work* 29, 6 (November–December 1984): 501–505.

Turner, J. "Predictors of Recidivism in Foster Care: Exploratory Models." *Social Work Research and Abstracts* 20, 2 (Summer 1984): 15–20.

Walton, E.; Fraser, M.W.; Lewis, R.E.; Pecora, P.J.; and Walton, W.K. "In-Home Family-Focused Reunification: An Experimental Study." *Child Welfare* LXXII, 5 (September–October 1993): 473–487.

Warsh, R.; Maluccio, A.N.; and Pine, B.A. *Teaching Family Reunification: A Sourcebook*. Washington, DC: Child Welfare League of America, 1993.

Werrbach, G.B. "The Family Reunification Role-Play." *Child Welfare* LXXII, 6 (November–December 1993): 555–568.

Whittaker, J.K.; Kinney, J.; Tracy, E.; and Booth, C., eds. *Reaching High-Risk Families: Intensive Family Preservation in the Human Services*. Hawthorne, NY: Aldine de Gruyter, 1990.

Wulczyn, F. "Caseload Dynamics and Foster Care Reentry." *Social Service Review* 65, 1 (March 1991): 133–156.

Yoskikami, R., et al. *Assessing the Implementation of Federal Policy to Reduce the Risk of Foster Care: Placement Prevention and Reunification in Child Welfare*. Portland, OR: Regional Research Institute for Human Services, Portland State University, 1983.

Family Preservation and Family-Centered Practice; Preventing Placement in Out-of-Home Care

Aldgate, J.; Pratt, R.; and Duggan, M. "Using Care Away from Home to Prevent Family Breakdown." *Adoption and Fostering* 13, 2 (1989): 32–37.

Barth, R.P. "Theories Guiding Home-Based Intensive Family Preservation Services." In *Reaching High-Risk Families: Intensive Family Preservation in Human Services*, edited by J.K. Whittaker, J. Kinney, E.M. Tracy, and C. Booth. Hawthorne, NY: Aldine de Gruyter, 1990, pp. 89–112.

Berry, M. "The Assessment of Imminence of Risk of Placement: Lessons from a Family Preservation Program." *Children and Youth Services Review* 13, 4 (1991): 239–256.

Bryce, M., and Lloyd, J.C., eds. *Treating Families in the Home: An Alternative to Placement*. Springfield, IL: Charles C Thomas, 1981.

Child Welfare League of America. *Standards for Services to Strengthen and Preserve Families with Children*. Washington, DC: Author, 1989.

Cole, E., and Duva, J. *Family Preservation: An Orientation for Administrators and Practitioners*. Washington, DC: Child Welfare League of America, 1990.

Compher, J. "Home Services to Families to Prevent Child Placement." *Social Work* 28, 5 (September–October 1983): 360–364.

Edna McConnell Clark Foundation. *Keeping Families Together: The Case for Family Preservation*. New York: Author, 1985.

Feldman, L. *Evaluating the Impact of Family Preservation Services in New Jersey*. Trenton, NJ: Bureau of Research, Evaluation and Quality Assurance, New Jersey Division of Youth and Family Services, 1990.

Frankel, Harvy. "Family-Centered, Home-Based Services in Child Protection: A Review of the Research." *Social Service Review* 62, 1 (March 1988): 137–157.

Fraser, M.W.; Pecora, P.J.; and Haapala, D.A., eds. *Families in Crisis: The Impact of Intensive Family Preservation Services*. New York: Aldine de Gruyter, 1991.

Haapala, D.A., and Kinney, J.M. "Avoiding Out-of-Home Placement of High-Risk Status Offenders Through the Use of Intensive Home-based Family Preservation Services." *Criminal Justice and Behavior* 15, 3 (March 1988): 334–348.

Haapala, D.A., and Kinney, J.M. "Homebuilders Approach to the Training of In-home Therapists." In *Home-Based Services for Children and Families: Policies, Practice, and Research*, edited by S. Maybanks and M.E. Bryce. Springfield, IL: Charles C Thomas, 1979.

Halper, G., and Jones, M.A. *Serving Families at Risk of Dissolution: Public Preventive Services in New York City*. New York: Human Resources Administration, 1981.

Halpern, R. "Home-Based Early Intervention: Dimensions of Current Practice." *Child Welfare* LXV, 4 (July–August 1986): 387–398.

Hartman, A., and Laird, J. *Family-Centered Social Work Practice*. New York: Free Press, 1983.

Haugaard, J.; Hokanson, B.; and National Resource Center on Family-Based Services. *Measuring the Cost-Effectiveness of Family-Based Services and Out-of-Home Care*. Oakdale, IA: National Clearinghouse for Family-Centered Programs, School of Social Work, University of Iowa, 1983.

Hinckley, E.C. "Homebuilders: The Maine Experience." *Children Today* 13, 5 (September–October 1984): 14–17.

Hutchinson, J., and Nelson, K. "How Public Agencies Can Provide Family-Centered Services." *Social Casework* 66, 6 (June 1985): pp. 367–371.

Hutchinson, J.; Lloyd, J.; Landsman, M.J.; Nelson, K.; and Bryce, M. *Family Centered Social Services: A Model for*

Child Welfare Agencies. Oakdale, IA: The National Resource Center on Family Based Services, University of Iowa, 1983.

Hutchison, E.D. "Use of Authority in Direct Social Work Practice with Mandated Clients." *Social Service Review* 61, 4 (December 1987): 581–598.

Jackson, S. *Intensive Family Services: A Family Preservation Service Model*. Baltimore, MD: Maryland Department of Human Resources, 1987.

Jones, M.A. *A Second Chance for Families: Five Years Later*. New York: Child Welfare League of America, 1985.

Kagan, S.L.; Powell, D.R.; Weissbourd, B.; and Zigler, E.F., eds. *America's Family Support Programs*. New Haven, CT: Yale University Press, 1987.

Kagan, R., and Schlosberg, S. *Families in Perpetual Crisis*. New York: W.W. Norton, 1989.

Kaplan, L. *Working with Multiproblem Families*. Lexington, MA: D.C Heath–Lexington Books, 1986.

Kinney, J.; Haapala, D.; and Booth, C. *Keeping Families Together*. Hawthorne, NY: Aldine de Gruyter, 1991.

Kinney, J.; Madsen, B.; Fleming, T.; and Haapala, D. "Homebuilders: Keeping Families Together." *Journal of Consulting and Clinical Psychology* 45, 4 (August 1977): 667–673.

Kinney, J.M. "Homebuilders: An In-home Crisis Intervention Program." *Children Today* 7, 1 (January-February 1978): 15–17, 35.

Kinney, J.; Haapala, D.; Booth, C.; and Leavitt, S. "The Homebuilders Model." In *Reaching High-Risk Families: Intensive Family Preservation in Human Services*, edited by J.K. Whittaker, J. Kinney, E.M. Tracy, and C. Booth. New York: Aldine de Gruyter, 1990, pp. 31–64.

Kinney, J.; Haapala, D.; and Gast, J.E. "Assessment of Families in Crisis." In *Treating Families in the Home*, edited by M. Bryce and J. Lloyd. Springfield, IL: Charles C Thomas, 1981.

Lipton, Linda. "Family Resource Programs." *Children Today* 12, 5 (September–October 1983): 11–13.

Lloyd, J.C., and Bryce, M.E. *Placement Prevention and Family Reunification: A Handbook for the Family-Centered Practitioner* (rev.). Iowa City, IA: National Resource Center on Family Based Services, The University of Iowa School of Social Work, 1984.

Maluccio, A.N. "Family Preservation Services and the Social Work Practice Sequence." In *Reaching High-Risk Families: Intensive Family Preservation in Human Services*, edited by J.K. Whittaker, J. Kinney, E.M. Tracy, and C. Booth. New York: Aldine de Gruyter, 1990, pp. 113–126.

Maluccio, A.N. "Research Perspectives on Social Support Systems for Families and Children." *Journal of Applied Social Sciences* 13, 2 (Spring/Summer 1989): 269–292.

Mannes, M., ed. *Family Preservation and Indian Child Welfare*. Albuquerque, NM: American Indian Law Center, Inc., 1990.

Maybanks, S., and Bryce, M.E., eds. *Home-Based Services for Children and Families: Policy, Practice, and Research*. Springfield, IL: Charles C Thomas, 1979.

Miller, K.; Fein, E.; Howe, G.; Gaudio, C.; and Bishop, G. "A Parent-Aide Program: Recordkeeping, Outcomes, and Costs." *Child Welfare* LXIV, 4 (July–August 1985): 407–419.

Miller, K.; Fein, E.; Howe, G.; Gaudio, C.; and Bishop, G. "Time Limited Goal-Focused Parent Aide Services." *Social Casework* 65, 8 (October 1984): 472–477.

National Resource Center on Family-Based Services. *Family-Centered Social Services: A Model for Child Welfare Agencies*. Oakdale, IA: Author, 1983.

Nelson, K.E.; Landsman, M.J.; and Detelbaum, W. "Three Models of Family-Centered Placement Prevention Services." *Child Welfare* LXIX, 1 (January–February 1990): 3–21.

Pecora, P.J.; Fraser, M.W.; Haapala, D.; and Bartolome, J.A. *Defining Family Preservation Services: Three Intensive Home-Based Treatment Programs*. Salt Lake City, UT: Social Research Institute, Graduate School of Social Work, University of Utah, 1987.

Rossi, P.H. *Evaluating Family Preservation Programs: A Report to the Edna McConnell Clark Foundation*. New York: Edna McConnell Clark Foundation, 1991.

Sherman, F.A.; Neumann, R.; and Shyne, A.W. *Children Adrift in Foster Care: A Study of Alternative Approaches*. New York: Child Welfare League of America, 1974.

Smith, Teresa. "Family Centers: Prevention, Partnership, or Community Alternative?" In *Progress in Child Health* (vol. 3), edited by J.A. MacFarlane. London: Churchill Livingstone, 1987, pp. 176–189.

Stehno, S.M. "Family-Centered Child Welfare Services: New Life for a Historic Idea." *Child Welfare* LXV, 3 (May–June 1986): 231–240.

Stein, T.J. "Projects to Prevent Out-of-Home Placement." *Children and Youth Services Review* 7, 2/3 (1985): 109–121.

Stinnett, N.; Chesser, B.; DeFrain, J.; and Knaub, P. *Family Strengths: Positive Models for Family Life*. Lincoln, NE: University of Nebraska Press, 1980.

Sundel, M., and Homan, C.C. "Prevention in Child Welfare: A Framework for Management and Practice." Child Welfare LVIII, 8 (September–October 1979) 510–521.

Tracy, E.M; Haapala, D.A.; Kinney, J.; and Pecora, P.J. *Intensive Family Preservation Services: An Instructional Sourcebook*. Cleveland, OH: Case Western Reserve University, Mandel School of Applied Social Services, 1990.

Tracy, E.M., and Whittaker, J.K. "The Evidence Base for Social Support Interventions in Child and Family Practice: Emerging Issues for Research and Practice." *Children and Youth Services Review* 9, 4 (1987): 249–270.

Wald, M. "Family Preservation: Are We Moving Too Fast?" *Public Welfare* 46, 3 (Summer 1988): 33–38.

Wells, K., and Biegel, D.E., eds. *Family Preservation Services: Research and Evaluation*. Newbury Park, CA: Sage Publications, 1991.

Whittaker, J.K.; Kinney, J.; Tracy, E.M.; and Booth, C. *Reaching High-Risk Families: Intensive Family Preservation in Human Services*. Hawthorne, NY: Aldine de Gruyter, 1990).

Yuan, Y.Y., and Rivest, M., eds. *Evaluation Resources for Family Preservation Programs*. Newbury Park, CA: Sage Publications, 1990.

Permanency Planning

Barth, R.P., and Berry, M. "Outcomes of Child Welfare Services Under Permanency Planning." *Social Service Review* 61, 1 (March 1987): 71–90.

Barth, R.P., and Berry, M. "A Decade Later: Outcomes of Permanency Planning." In *The Adoption Assistance and Child Welfare Act of 1980: The First Ten Years*, edited by the North American Council on Adoptable Children. St. Paul, MN: The North American Council on Adoptable Children, 1990.

Downs, S., and Taylor, C., eds. *Permanent Planning in Foster Care: Resources for Training*. Washington, DC: U.S. Department of Health and Human Services, 1980.

Downs, S.; Bayless, L.; Dreyer, L.; Emlen, A.C.; Hardin, M.; Helm, L.; Lahti, J.; Liedtke, K.; Schimske, K.; and Troychak, M. *Foster Care Reform in the '70s: Final Report of the Permanency Planning Dissemination Project*. Portland, OR: Regional Research Institute for Human Services, Portland State University, 1981.

Dreyer, L. *Permanent Planning in Foster Care: A Guide for Program Planners*. Portland, OR: Regional Research

Institute for Human Services, Portland State University, 1978.

Emlen, A.; Lahti, J.; Downs, G.; McKay, A.; and Downs, S. *Overcoming Barriers to Planning for Children in Foster Care*. Portland, OR: Regional Research Institute for Human Services, Portland State University, 1977.

Fanshel, David. *On the Road to Permanency*. New York: Child Welfare League of America, 1982.

Gambrill, E., and Stein, T.J., eds. "Permanency Planning for Children." *Children and Youth Services Review* (Special Issue) 7, 2/3 (1985).

Howe, George. "The Ecological Approach to Permanency Planning: An Interactionist Perspective." *Child Welfare* LXII, 4 (April 1983): 291–301.

Jones, M., and Biesecker, J. *Permanency Planning Guide for Children and Youth Services*. Millersville, PA: Training Resources in Permanent Planning Project, Millersville State College, 1979.

Jones, M., and Biesecker, J. "Training in Permanency Planning: Using What is Known." *Child Welfare* LIX, 8 (September–October 1980): 481–490.

Lahti, J. "A Follow-up Study of Foster Children in Permanent Placements." *Social Service Review* 56, 4 (December 1982): 556–571.

Maluccio, A.N.; Fein, E.; Hamilton, V.J.; Klier, J.; and Ward, D. "Beyond Permanency Planning." *Child Welfare* LIX, 9 (November 1980): 515–530.

Maluccio, A.N., and Fein, E. "Permanency Planning: A Redefinition." *Child Welfare* LXII, 3 (May–June 1983): 195–201.

Maluccio, A.N., and Fein, E. "Permanency Planning Revisited." In *Foster Care: Current Issues, Policies, and Practices*, edited by M. Cox and R. Cox. Norwood, NJ: Ablex Press, 1985.

Maluccio, A.N.; Fein, E.; and Olmstead, K.A. *Permanency Planning for Children: Concepts and Methods*. London and New York: Tavistock Publications and Methuen, Inc., 1986.

Olmstead, K.A.; Hamilton, J.; and Fein, E. "Permanency Planning for Children in Outpatient Psychiatric Services.". In *Advances in Clinical Social Work*, edited by C.B. Germain. Silver Spring, MD: National Association of Social Workers, 1985.

Pelton, L.L. "Beyond Permanency Planning: Restructuring the Public Child Welfare System." *Social Work* 36, 4 (April 1991): 337–343.

Pike, V. "Permanent Families for Foster Children: The Oregon Project." *Children Today* 5,6 (November–December 1976): 22–25.

Pike, V.; Downs, S.; Emlen, A.; Downs, G.; and Case, D. *Permanent Planning for Children in Foster Care: A Handbook for Social Workers*. Washington, DC: U.S. Department of Health, Education, and Welfare, Publication No. (OHDS) 78–30124, 1977.

Rooney, R.H. "Permanency Planning: Boon for All Children?" *Social Work* 27, 2 (March 1982): 152–158.

Seaberg, J.R. "Reasonable Efforts: Toward Implementation in Permanency Planning." *Child Welfare* LXV, 5 (September–October 1986): 469–479.

Seltzer, M.M., and Bloksberg, L.M. "Permanency Planning and its Effects on Foster Children." *Social Work* 32, 1 (January–February 1987): 65–68.

Soskin, M. "Delivering Services Under Permanency Planning." *Social Service Review* 61, 2 (June 1987): 272–290.

Ten Broeck, E., and Barth, R.P. "Learning the Hard Way: A Pilot Permanency Planning Project." *Child Welfare* LXV, 3 (May–June 1986): 281–294.

Thoburn, J.; Murdoch, A.; and O'Brien, A. *Permanence in Child Care*. Oxford: Basil Blackwell, 1986.

Race and Ethnicity

Billingsley, A., and Giovannoni, J.M. *Children of the Storm: Black Children and American Child Welfare*. New York: Harcourt Brace Jovanovich, 1970.

Boyd-Franklin, N. *Black Families in Therapy—A Multisystems Approach*. New York: The Guilford Press, 1989.

Chestang, L.W. "The Delivery of Child Welfare Services to Minority Group Children and Their Families." In *Child Welfare Strategy in the Coming Years*. Washington, DC: U.S. Department of Health, Education, and Welfare, Publication No. (OHDS) 78–30158, 1978, pp. 169–194.

Green, J.W. *Cultural Awareness in Human Services*. Englewood Cliffs, NJ: Prentice-Hall, 1982.

Hill, R. *Informal Adoption Among Black Families*. Washington, DC: National Urban League, 1976.

Ho, M.K. *Family Therapy with Ethnic Minorities*. Newbury Park, CA: Sage Publications, 1987.

Ho, M.K. *Minority Children and Adolescents in Therapy*. Newbury Park, CA: Sage Publications, 1992.

Hogan, P.T., and Siu, S.F. "Minority Children and the Child Welfare System: An Historical Perspective." *Social Work* 33, 6 (November–December 1988): 493–498.

Jacobs, C., and Bowles, D.D., eds. *Ethnicity and Race—Critical Concepts for Social Work*. Silver Spring, MD: National Association of Social Workers, 1988.

Leon, A.M.; Mazur, R.; Montalvo, E.; and Rodrieguez, M. "Self-Help Support Groups for Hispanic Mothers." *Child Welfare* LXIII, 4 (May–June 1984) 261–268.

McGoldrick, M.; Pearce, J.K.; and Giordano, J. *Ethnicity and Family Therapy*. New York: The Guilford Press, 1982.

Olsen, Lenore. "Services for Minority Children in Out-of-Home Care." *Social Service Review* 56, 4 (December 1982): 572–585.

Pinderhughes, E. *Understanding Race, Ethnicity, and Power*. New York: The Free Press, 1989.

Pinderhughes, E.E. "The Delivery of Child Welfare Services to African American Clients." *American Journal of Orthopsychiatry* 61, 4 (October 1991): 599–605.

Stehno, S.M. "Differential Treatment of Minority Children in Service Systems." *Social Work* 27, 1 (January 1982): 39–46.

Walker, F.C. "Cultural and Ethnic Issues in Working with Black Families in the Child Welfare System." In *Parents of Children in Placement: Perspectives and Programs*, edited by P.A. Sinanoglu and A.N. Maluccio. New York: Child Welfare League of America, 1981, pp. 133–148.

Child Maltreatment

Physical and Emotional Abuse and Neglect

Brown, L. "The Future of Child Protection Services: Seeking a National Consensus." *Public Welfare* 45, 1 (Winter 1987): 12–17.

Daro, D. *Confronting Child Abuse—Research for Effective Program Design*. New York: Free Press, 1988.

Ebeling, N.B., and Hill, D.A., eds. *Child Abuse and Neglect: A Guide for Case Studies for Treating the Child and Family*. Boston: John Wright—PSG, 1983.

Faller, K.C., ed. *Social Work with Abused and Neglected Children: A Manual of Interdisciplinary Practice*. New York: Free Press, 1981.

Garbarino, J., and Gilliam, G. *Understanding Abusive Families*. Lexington, MA: Lexington Books, 1980.

Lystad, M. *Violence in the Home: Interdisciplinary Perspectives*. New York: Brunner/Mazel, 1986.

Miller, J.L., and Whittaker, J.K. "Social Services and Social

Support: Blended Programs for Families at Risk of Child Maltreatment." *Child Welfare* LXVII, 2 (March–April 1988): 161–174.

Nelson, B.J. *Making an Issue of Child Abuse: Political Agenda Setting for Social Problems*. Chicago: University of Chicago Press, 1984.

Pelton, L.H. ed. *The Social Context of Child Abuse and Neglect*. New York: Human Sciences Press, 1981.

Tower, C. *Understanding Child Abuse and Neglect*. Needham Heights, MA: Allyn and Bacon, 1989.

Wald, M.S.; Carlsmith, J.M.; and Leiderman, P.H. *Protecting Abused and Neglected Children*. Stanford, CA: Stanford University Press, 1988.

Sexual Abuse

Conte, J.R. "An Evaluation of a Program to Prevent Sexual Victimization of Young Children." *Child Abuse and Neglect* 9, 3 (1985): 319–328.

Conte, J.R.; Wolf, S.; and Smith, T. "What Sexual Offenders Tell Us About Prevention Strategies." *Child Abuse and Neglect* 13, 3 (Fall 1989): 293–301.

Finkelhor, D. Child *Sexual Abuse—New Theory and Research*. New York: Free Press, 1984.

Finkelhor, D.; Araji, S.; Baron, L.; Browne, A.; Peters, S.D.; and Wyatt, G.E. *A Sourcebook on Child Sexual Abuse*. Beverly Hills, CA: Sage Publications, 1986.

Groth, A.N. "Treatment of the Sexual Offender in a Correctional Institution." In *The Sexual Aggressor—Current Perspectives on Treatment*, edited by J.G. Greer and I.R. Stuart. New York: Van Nostrand Reinhold, 1983.

Haugaard, J.J., and Reppucci, N.D. *The Sexual Abuse of Children*. San Francisco: Jossey–Bass, 1988.

Hollin, C.R., and Howells, K., eds. *Clinical Approaches to Sex Offenders and Their Victims*. New York: John Wiley, 1991.

McFarlane, K. and Waterman, J., with Conerly, S.; Damon, L.; Durfee, M.; and Long, S. *Sexual Abuse of Young Children*. New York: Guilford Press, 1986.

Pecora, P.J.; Whittaker, J.K.; and Maluccio, A.N. "Sexual Abuse: Prevention and Treatment." In *The Child Welfare Challenge: Policy, Practice and Research*, by P.J. Pecora, J.K. Whittaker, and A.N. Maluccio. New York: Aldine de Gruyter, 1992.

Sgroi, S., ed. *Handbook of Clinical Intervention in Child Sexual Abuse*. Lexington, MA: Lexington Books, 1982.

Adoption

Barth, R., ed. "Research on Special Needs Adoption." *Children and Youth Services Review* (Special Issue) 13, 5/6 (1991).

Barth, R.P., and Berry, M. *Adoption and Disruption: Rates, Risks, and Responses.* New York: Aldine de Gruyter (1988).

Berry, M. "The Effects of Open Adoption on Biological and Adoptive Parents and the Children: The Arguments and the Evidence." *Child Welfare* LXX, 6 (November–December 1991): 637–651.

Brodzinsky, D.M., and Schechter, M.D., eds. *The Psychology of Adoption.* New York: Oxford University Press, 1990.

Churchill, S.R.; Carlson, B.; and Nybell, L., eds. *No Child is Unadoptable: A Reader on Adoption of Children with Special Needs.* Beverly Hills, CA: Sage Publications, 1979.

Coleman, L.; Tilbor, K.; Hornby, E.; and Boggis, C., eds. *Working with Older Adoptees—A Sourcebook of Innovative Models.* Portland, ME: University of Southern Maine, 1988.

DeWoody, M. *Adoption and Disclosure: A Review of the Law.* Washington, DC: Child Welfare League of America, 1993.

Feigelman, W., and Silverman, A. *Chosen Children: New Patterns of Adoption Relationships.* New York: Praeger, 1983.

Gill, O., and Jackson, B. *Adoption and Race.* London and New York: Batsford Academic/St. Martin's Press, 1983.

Grow, L.J., and Shapiro, D. *Black Children—White Parents: A Study of Transracial Adoption.* New York: Child Welfare League of America, 1974.

Hartman, Ann. *Working with Adoptive Families Beyond Placement.* New York: Child Welfare League of America, 1984.

Jewett, Claudia. *Adopting the Older Child.* Cambridge, MA: Harvard Common Press, 1978.

Kirk, H.D. *Adoptive Kinship.* New York: Free Press, 1981.

McRoy, R.G.; Grotevant, H.D.; and Zurcher, L.A. *Emotional Disturbance in Adopted Adolescents: Origins and Development.* New York: Praeger, 1988.

McRoy, R.G.; Grotevant, H.D.; and Shite, K.L. *Openness in Adoption: New Practices, New Issues.* New York: Praeger, 1988.

Meezan, W., and Shireman, J.F. *Care and Commitment—Foster Parent Adoption Decisions.* Albany, NY: State University of New York Press, 1985.

Pine, B.A. *Special Families for Special Children: The Adoption of Children with Developmental Disabilities.* Unpublished doctoral dissertation, Brandeis University, 1991.

Rodriguez, P., and Meyer, A.S. "Minority Adoptions and Agency Practices." *Social Work* 35, 6 (November 1990): 528–531.

Sachdev, P., ed. *Adoption: Current Issues and Trends.* Toronto, ON: Butterworth and Co., 1984.

Sachdev, P. *Unlocking the Adoption Files.* Lexington, MA: Lexington Books, 1989.

Simon, R.J., and Alstein, H. *Transracial Adoptees and Their Families.* New York: Praeger, 1987.

Sorosky, A.D.; Baran, A.: and Panner, R. *The Adoption Triangle.* New York: Doubleday, 1978.

Triseliotis, J., ed. *New Developments in Foster Care and Adoption.* London: Routledge and Kegan Paul, 1980.

Group Care/Residential Treatment

Abramczyk, L.W., ed. *Residential Child Care in England and the Carolinas: Challenges and Opportunities.* Columbia, SC: University of South Carolina, Center for Child and Family Studies, 1990.

Ainsworth, F., and Fulcher, L.C., eds. *Group Care for Children: Concepts and Issues.* London and New York: Tavistock Publications, 1981.

Ainsworth, F. "A 'No Blame' Approach to Work with Families of Children and Adolescents in Residential Care." *Child and Youth Care Forum* 20, 5 (October 1991): 301–311.

Beker, J. and Eisikovits, Z., eds. *Knowledge Utilization in Residential Child and Youth Care Practice.* Washington, DC: Child Welfare League of America, 1991.

Carman, G.O., and Small, R.W., eds. *Permanence and Support: Changing Practice in Group Child Care.* Washington, DC: Child Welfare League of America, 1988.

Kelsall, J., and McCullough, B. *Family Work in Residential Child Care: Partnership in Practice.* Cheadle, England: Boys' and Girls' Welfare Society, 1988.

Maier, H.W. *Developmental Group Care of Children and Youth.* New York: Haworth Press, 1988.

Schaefer, C.E., and Swanson, A.J., eds. *Children in Residential Care: Critical Issues in Treatment.* New York: Van Nostrand Reinhold, 1988.

Wells, K. "Eagerly Awaiting a Home: Severely Emotionally

Disturbed Youth Lost in our Systems of Care." *Child and Youth Care Forum*, 20, 1 (February 1991): 7–18.

Whittaker, J.K. *Caring for Troubled Children: Residential Treatment in a Community Context*. San Francisco: Jossey-Bass, 1979.

Whittaker, J.K. "Family Involvement in Residential Treatment: A Support System for Parents." In *The Challenge of Partnership: Working with Parents of Children in Foster Care*, edited by A.N. Maluccio and P.A. Sinanoglu. New York: Child Welfare League of America, 1981, pp. 67–88.

Whittaker, J.K., and Maluccio, A.N. "Understanding the Families of Children in Foster and Residential Care." In *Troubled Relationships*, edited by E.W. Nunnally, C.S. Chilman, and F.M. Cox. Newbury Park, CA: Sage Publications, 1988, pp. 192–204.

Family Foster Care

Aldgate, J. and Hawley, D. *Recollections of Disruption—A Study of Foster Care Breakdowns*. London: National Foster Care Association, 1986.

Berridge, D., and Cleaver, H. *Foster Home Breakdown*. Oxford: Basil Blackwell, 1987.

Blumenthal, K., and Weinberg, A., eds. *Establishing Parent Involvement in Foster Care Agencies*. New York: Child Welfare League of America, 1984.

Cahn, K. and Johnson, P., eds. *Children Can't Wait: Reducing Delays for Children in Foster Care*. Washington, DC: Child Welfare League of America, 1993.

Cox, M., and Cox, R., eds. *Foster Care: Current Issues, Policies, and Practices*. Norwood, NJ: Ablex Press, 1985.

DiBerto, G.W. "An Outlook for Foster Care in the United States." *Child Welfare* LXIX, 1 (January–February 1990): 75–81.

Eastman, K.S. "Foster Families: A Comprehensive Bibliography." *Child Welfare* LXIV, 6 (November–December 1985): 565–585.

Fanshel, D., and Shinn, E.B. *Children in Foster Care—A Longitudinal Investigation*. New York: Columbia University Press, 1978.

Fanshel, D.; Finch, S.J.; and Grundy, J.F. *Foster Children in a Life Course Perspective*. New York: Columbia University Press, 1990.

Fein, E. "Issues in Foster Family Care: Where Do We Stand?" *American Journal of Orthopsychiatry* 61, 4 (October 1991): 578–583.

Fein, E., and Maluccio, A.N. "Foster Family Care: Solution or Problem?" In *Why Some Children Succeed Despite the Odds*, edited by W.A. Rhodes and W.K. Brown. New York: Praeger, 1991.

Galaway, B.; Maglajlic, D.; Hudson, J.; Harmon, P.; and McLagan, J., eds. *International Perspectives on Specialist Foster Family Care*. St. Paul, MN: Human Service Associates, 1990.

Fein, E.; Maluccio, A.N.; Hamilton, V.J.; and Ward, D. "After Foster Care: Outcomes of Permanency Planning for Children." *Child Welfare* LXII, 6 (November–December 1983): 485–558.

Fein, E.; Maluccio, A.N.; and Kluger, M. *No More Partings: An Examination of Long-Term Foster Family Care*. Washington, DC: Child Welfare League of America, 1990.

Hardin, M., ed. *Foster Children in the Courts*. Boston: Butterworth Legal Publishers, 1983.

Hawkins, R.P., and Breiling, J., eds. *Therapeutic Foster Care: Critical Issues*. Washington, DC: Child Welfare League of America, 1989.

Hess, P.M., and Proch, K.O. *Family Visiting in Out-of-Home Care: A Guide to Practice*. Washington, DC: Child Welfare League of America, 1988.

Horejsi, C.R.; Bertsche, A.V.; and Clark, F.W. *Social Work Practice with Parents of Children in Foster Care: A Handbook*. Springfield, IL: Charles C Thomas, 1981.

Hudson, J., and Galaway, B., eds. *Specialist Foster Family Care: A Normalizing Experience*. New York: The Haworth Press, 1989.

Kates, W.G.; Johnson, R.L.; Rader, M.W.; and Strieder, F.H. "Whose Child Is This? Assessment and Treatment of Children in Foster Care." *American Journal of Orthopsychiatry* 61, 4 (October 1991): 584–591.

Lee, J.A.B., and Nisivoccia, D. *Walk a Mile in My Shoes—A Book About Biological Parents for Foster Parents and Social Workers*. Washington, DC: Child Welfare League of America, 1989.

Lindsey, D. "Factors Affecting the Foster Care Placement Decision: An Analysis of National Survey Data." *American Journal of Orthopsychiatry* 61, 2 (April 1991): 272–281.

Maluccio, A.N., and Sinanoglu, P.A., eds. *The Challenge of Partnership: Working with Parents of Children in Foster Care*. New York: Child Welfare League of America, 1981.

Maluccio, A.N., and Whittaker, J.K. "Helping the Biological Families of Children in Out-of-Home Placement." In *Troubled Relationships*, edited by W.W. Nunnally, C.S.

Chilman, and F.M. Cox. Newbury Park, CA: Sage Publications, 1988, pp. 205–217.

Maluccio, A.N.; Fein, E.; and Olmstead, K.A. *Permanency Planning for Children—Concepts and Methods*. London and New York: Tavistock and Methuen, 1986.

Molin, R. "Future Anxiety: Clinical Issues of Children in the Latter Phases of Foster Care." *Child and Adolescent Social Work* 7, 6 (December 1990): 501–512.

National Commission on Family Foster Care. *A Blueprint for Fostering Infants, Children, and Youths in the 1990s*. Washington, DC: Child Welfare League of America, 1991.

Pelton, L.H. "Not for Poverty Alone: Foster Care Population Trends in the 20th Century." *Journal of Sociology and Social Welfare* 14, 2 (February 1987): 37–62.

Rowe, J.; Cain, H.; Hundleby, M., and Keane, A. *Long-Term Foster Care*. London: Batsford/BAAF, 1984.

Rowe, J.; Hundleby, M.; and Garnett, L. *Child Care Now: A Survey of Placement Patterns*. London: British Agencies for Adoption and Fostering, 1989.

Schatz, M.S., and Bane, W. "Empowering the Parents of Children in Substitute Care: A Training Model." *Child Welfare* LXX, 6 (November–December1991): 665–678.

Sinanoglu, P.A., and Maluccio, A.N., eds. *Parents of Children in Placement: Perspectives and Programs*. New York: Child Welfare League of America, 1981.

Simms, M.D. "The Foster Care Clinic: A Community Program to Identify Treatment Needs of Children in Foster Care." *Journal of Developmental and Behavioral Pediatrics* 10, 4 (June 1989): 121–128.

Stein, M., and Carey, K. *Leaving Care*. Oxford, England: Basil Blackwell, 1986.

Stein, T.J.; Gambrill, E.D.; and Wiltse, K.T. *Children in Foster Homes—Achieving Continuity of Care*. New York: Praeger Publishers, 1978.

Thomas, C. "The Resolution of Object Loss following Foster Home Placement." *Smith College Studies in Social Work* 37, 3 (June 1967): 163–234.

Triseliotis, J., ed. *New Developments in Foster Care and Adoption*. London: Routledge and Kegan, Paul, 1980.

Adolescents and Independent Living

Aldgate, J.; Maluccio, A.; and Reeves, C. *Adolescents in Foster Families*. London: B.T. Batsford, and Chicago: Lyceum Books, 1989.

Ansell, D. *Making It On Your Own*. Richmond, VA: Region Resource Center for Children, Youth, and Families, School of Social Work, Virginia Commonwealth University, 1983.

Barth, R. "Emancipation Services for Adolescents in Foster Care." *Social Work* 31, 3 (May–June 1986): 165–171.

DeWoody, M.; Ceja, K.; and Sylvester, M. *Independent Living Services for Youths in Out-of-Home Care*. Washington, DC: Child Welfare League of America, 1993.

Festinger, T. *No One Ever Asked Us...A Postscript to Foster Care*. New York: Columbia University Press, 1983.

Griffin, W.V. *Independent Living Strategies—A Program to Prepare Adolescents for their Exit from Foster or Group Care (2nd ed.)*. Tulsa, OK: National Resource Center for Youth Services, The University of Oklahoma, 1987.

Maluccio, A.N., and Fein, E. "Growing Up in Foster Care." *Children and Youth Services Review* 7, 2/3 (1985): 123–134.

Maluccio, A.N.; Krieger, R.; and Pine, B.A., eds. *Preparing Adolescents for Life After Foster Care: The Central Role of Foster Parents*. Washington, DC: Child Welfare League of America, 1990.

Mech, E., ed. *Independent-Living Services for At-Risk Adolescents*. Washington, DC: Child Welfare League of America, 1988 (special issue of the *Child Welfare* journal).

Meisels, S.B.; Jacobs, M.; and Rendeiro, E. *Decisions, Decisions, Decisions! Preparing for Young Adulthood! A Guide to Making Decisions That Work for You*. Tulsa, OK: National Resource Center for Youth Services and Boston, MA: Judge Baker Children's Center, 1988.

Pasztor, E.M.; Clarren, J.; Timberlake, E.M.; and Bayless, L. "Stepping Out of Foster Care into Independent Living." *Children Today* (March/April 1986).

Pasztor, E.M.; Polowy, M.E.; Wasson, D.L.; Wolf, M.; Krieger, R.; Jacobs, M.; and Green, R.K. *Preparing Youth for Interdependent Living—A Training Program for Foster Parents, Child Care Workers, and Social Workers*. Atlanta, GA: Child Welfare Institute, and West Hartford, CT: The University of Connecticut School of Social Work, 1987.

Ryan, P.; Rice, D.L.; and McFadden, E.J. *P-U-S-H for Youth G-O-A-L-S: Providing Understanding, Support, and Help for Youth Going Out and Living Successfully*. Ypsilanti, MI: Institute for the Study of Children and Families, Eastern Michigan University, 1987.

Sims, A.R. "Independent Living Services for Youths in Foster Care." *Social Work* 33, 6 (November–December 1988): 539–542.

Stein, M., and Carey, K. *Leaving Care*. Oxford, England: Basil Blackwell, 1986.

Stone, H.D. *Ready, Set, Go: An Agency Guide to Independent Living*. Washington, DC: Child Welfare League of America, 1987.

Susser, E.; Struening, E.L.; and Conover, S. "Childhood Experiences of Homeless Men." *American Journal of Psychiatry* 144, 12 (December 1987): 1599–1601.